D0049194

No Joke

LIBRARY OF JEWISH IDEAS

Cosponsored by the Tikvah Fund

The series presents engaging and authoritative treatments of core Jewish concepts in a form appealing to general readers who are curious about Jewish treatments of key areas of human thought and experience.

No Joke

Making Jewish Humor

Ruth R. Wisse

PRINCETON UNIVERSITY PRESS

Princeton and Oxford

Published by Princeton University Press, 41 William Street,
Princeton, New Jersey 08540
In the United Kingdom: Princeton University Press, 6 Oxford Street,
Woodstock, Oxfordshire OX20 1TW

press.princeton.edu

Library of Congress Cataloging-in-Publication Data

Wisse, Ruth R., author.
No joke : making Jewish humor / Ruth R. Wisse.
pages cm. – (Library of Jewish ideas)
Includes bibliographical references and index.
ISBN 978-0-691-14946-2 (alk. paper)
1. Jewish wit and humor—History and criticism. 2. Jews—Humor—History and criticism. I. Title.
PN6149.J4W49 2013
809.7′98924–dc23 2012051631

British Library Cataloging-in-Publication Data is available

Publication of this book has been aided by the Tikvah Fund

This book has been composed in Garamond Premiere and Tekton

Printed on acid-free paper. ∞

Printed in the United States of America

10 9 8 7 6 5 4 3 2 1

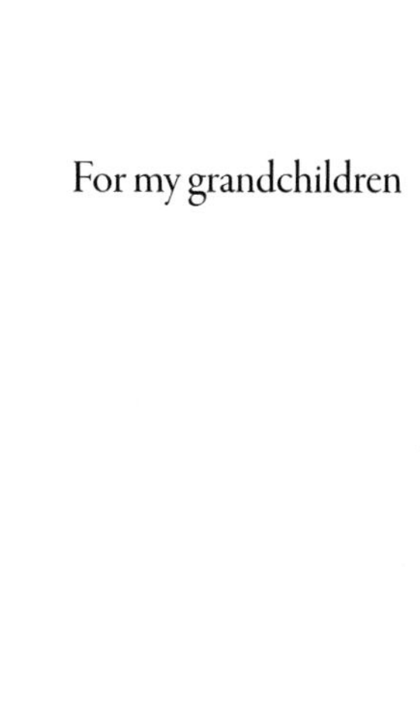

For my grandchildren

Contents

Illustrations

No Joke

Introduction

The Best Medicine

One morning, in Harvard's Semitic Museum where the Jewish Studies program is housed, I ran into two of my colleagues collecting their mail. The evening before, when I had lectured at a synagogue, a member of the audience had told me a good joke. I couldn't wait to share it:

> Four Europeans go hiking together and get terribly lost. First they run out of food, then out of water.
>
> "I'm so thirsty," says the Englishman. "I must have tea!"
>
> "I'm so thirsty," says the Frenchman. "I must have wine."
>
> "I'm so thirsty," says the German. "I must have beer."
>
> "I'm so thirsty," says the Jew. "I must have diabetes."

The joke was brand new when I told it that morning—though it is by now well worn, at least in part because I put it into circulation in published and recorded talks about Jewish humor. If you are into such things, you will appreciate my thrill at the laughter that greeted the punch line. How often do you get to tell Jews a joke that they haven't heard before?

But as I was about to follow my colleagues out of the front office, the receptionist, who had overheard our conversation, told me that she found the joke offensive. Indeed, if we weren't Jews, she said, she would have called it anti-Semitic. Could I please explain what was funny about it and account for our hilarity?

This young woman, let me call her Samantha, was dating a Jewish student in our department, and as a Gentile, had previously asked me about unfamiliar terms and concepts in the novels of Isaac Bashevis Singer. Hence I took my time in reassuring her that stereotypes are a regular feature of joking, which depends for its effect on brevity. With no time for elucidation, jokes often designate people by a single characteristic. Is it fair that Poles or "Newfies" (Newfoundlanders) get labeled as dumb? Are all Scots stingy? Are all mothers-in-law hateful? Because compression of this kind is essential to the genre, a single national association represents each of the hikers in the joke, and whichever of them was placed last in a serial buildup would invariably be at variance with the others. As the last of the four, the Jew was *expected* to say something different.

But this did not yet seem to get to the heart of the matter, so I continued: The joke turns on the double meaning of the verb "to have": (a) to possess, as in, to have a drink, and (b) to be afflicted by or have a disease. Repetition of the first usage by the Englishman, the Frenchman, and the German raises the expectation that the verb will continue to be used in the same way. When the Jew breaks the pattern, we laugh at the displacement of one anxiety (thirst) by a graver one (illness); Sigmund Freud provides a superb analysis of this technique in *Jokes and Their Relation to the Unconscious*. While the three hikers react to the problem at hand, the Jew anticipates its direst implications. The three want to quench their thirst, and he looks for complications behind the presumably obvious cause. Is he neurotic? A hypochondriac? Why is he conditioned for disaster? The joke may "know" what happened to the Jews of Europe and may assume that a Jew in European company is entitled to worry about his prospects of survival.

Forced in this way to think about the joke, I realized how it replicated the Jew's anxiety. A Jew in mixed European company introduces an additional level of insecurity beyond the one involved in the hike. Many times I had stood in that very building with those same colleagues discussing a recent suicide bombing in Israel or trading stories about our relatives in some hostile climate. The Jewish hiker's exaggerated worry made us laugh at a truth so ingeniously exposed. The joke organized our analogous concern and then exploded it to our surprised satisfaction.

I confess that my first impulse when Samantha asked me to explain the joke had been to tell her the famous one that introduces a collection of Yiddish humor by the folklorist Immanuel Olsvanger:

> When you tell a joke to a peasant, he laughs three times, once when you tell it to him, the second time when you explain it to him, and the third time when he understands it.

The landowner laughs twice. Once when you tell it to him and again when you explain it, because he never understands it.

The policeman laughs only once when you tell it to him, because he doesn't let you explain it so he never understands it.

When you tell a Jew a joke, he says, "I've heard it before. And I can tell it better."[1]

This joke ridicules those who don't get Jewish humor, in a pecking order of wit that is dominated by Jews to such a degree that their only competition is among themselves. Failure to laugh at a joke signifies something like dimness in the peasant, remoteness in the landowner, and severity in the police officer. The slowest to laugh is the most threatening, and the one who laughs soonest is the most human. If the Jew fails to laugh, it is not, God forbid, because he missed the point of the joke but because he has exhausted the fund of laughter. The joke uses humor as a touchstone of humanity, consigning those who lack it to some lower existence, but implying that Jews are almost too human for their own good.

Naturally, I didn't tell Sam this joke because it might have expanded the distance between us that we were trying to shrink. The Olsvanger joke, if I may call it that, assumes an adversarial relation between Gentiles and Jews. It suited European societies where Christian peasants, landowners, and police were often hostile to Jews; intended solely for those who spoke the Jewish language, it was told elsewhere in Europe about an Englishman, a Frenchman, and a German. The antagonism of surrounding European societies made Jews eager for the only kind of payback they could afford to indulge. But as far as I know, the joke has no U.S. equivalent. Who would be its foils? Blacks, Hispanics, and WASPs? A bank teller, manager, and president? There may be plenty of ethnic and racial joking in the United States, and some anti-Jewish bigotry behind it, but nowadays East and West Coast Americans seem so familiar with Jewish comedy that I was frankly surprised Samantha did not join in our laughter. Had I thought the joke excluded her, I might not have told it in that semipublic space.

Sam seems to me like the kindly bystander who worries about the health of smokers. She wants to protect Jews from anti-Semitism, which she associates with whatever sets them apart. In her eagerness to draw us all together, she may fail to understand why we should accept, reinforce, and celebrate our peculiarity. So does Sam have a point? Is it appropriate to wonder why Jews should enjoy laughing at themselves? Why joking acquired such value in Jewish society, or why Yiddish—the language of European Jewry, whose culture I teach at the university—is thought to be inherently funny?

As it happens, joking had also figured at a faculty meeting a few weeks earlier—though lest you think this is what we do all day, let me say that I found such occasions memorable because they were rare. The senior faculty of Harvard's Department of Near Eastern Languages and Civilizations, which includes Jewish Studies, Arabic, Armenian, Turkish, and Persian as well as the languages and archaeology of the ancient Near East, had gathered to vote on a new professorial position. We had been looking so long for the "right person" that the dean was threatening to cancel the search if we did not immediately arrive at a decision. Our chair, who had also reached the limits of his patience, said he wanted a unanimous vote on our likeliest candidate, and that he would go around the table asking everyone either to agree or object with cause. The positive votes were adding up nicely until it came to our most demanding colleague, who had blocked some of the earlier applicants. He paused for a moment, then sighed and said, "Well, I guess he passes the Rosenberg test." The non-Jewish members looked expectantly to us Jews, but we hadn't a clue what this meant. Our colleague explained:

> Mrs. Rosenberg goes to the butcher early Friday morning to buy her usual chicken for sabbath and begins her usual routine of inspection. She is not satisfied with an examination from across the counter, but asks the butcher to hand her the bird. She lifts each wing and sniffs suspiciously, then one leg at a time, and finally the orifice. The butcher, who has tired of this performance, says, "Frankly, Mrs. Rosenberg, I don't know which of *us* could pass your test!"

The laughter that greeted this punch line sealed the decision. The fastidious colleague had told the joke at his own expense to expose the folly of excessive inspection. The mention of a Jewish-sounding name had raised expectations of some special Jewish wisdom only to dash them in a joke that was equally accessible to all. Implicitly, the laughter uniting us even included the prospective department member who had just been voted into our ranks.

These two examples of Jewish joking seem alike in making fun of Jews themselves, yet the ecumenicism of the second differs from the particularism of the first. Mrs. Rosenberg could have been Mrs. O'Brien stalking a Christmas turkey with no sacrifice of comic outcome, whereas the Jew's concern about diabetes spoofed some allegedly *Jewish* trait. The Jewish-sounding name that threatened to distinguish Jews from non-Jews in the Rosenberg joke was only part of the diversionary machinery that kept attention on the action until the final shift of focus, whereas in the hikers' joke the Jew was at once the target and audience. Here we see that even within the same academic department, Jewish joking can function in opposing ways to include and exclude different constituencies. How much more so in the geographically and linguistically divergent communities this book explores.

■ Most of its aficionados take a positive view of Jewish joking. "Incidentally," writes Freud, one of its devotees, "I do not know whether there are many other instances of a people making fun to such a degree of its own character."[2] He writes this approvingly, adducing an example of Jewish self-deprecation:

> A Galician Jew was traveling by train, and had made himself really comfortable, had unbuttoned his coat and put his feet up on the seat. [The regional designation here signifies traditionalism and lack of deportment.] Just then a gentleman in modern dress entered the compartment. The Galitsyaner promptly pulled himself together and took up a proper pose. The stranger fingered through the

> pages of a notebook, made some calculations, reflected for a moment and then suddenly asked the other: "Excuse me, when is Yom Kippur?" "Oho!" said our traveler, putting his feet up on the seat again as he answered.[3]

Freud thinks this anecdote conveys the Jews' democratic mode of thinking, "which recognizes no distinction between lords and serfs, but also, alas, upsets discipline and co-operation."[4] The joke reinforces the stereotype of the uncouth traditional Jew that exists in the mind of Gentiles, but redeems the indictment through the egalitarian spirit it uncovers among the Jews themselves. One may say the same of the analyst telling the joke. Freud, too, is relaxing, putting up his feet, indifferent to the impression he is making because he assumes that the others in his "compartment" of listeners or readers resemble him in finding it funny. (Regarding this intimacy, Theodor Reik, a member of Freud's Vienna Psychoanalytic Society, recalls the quip of a fellow member at the appearance of Ernest Jones, one of the only non-Jews in their circle: "*Barukh atoh adonoy*, here comes the honor-Goy.")[5]

But Freud's contemporary Arthur Schnitzler treated Freud's joke much more guardedly. In Schnitzler's novel *Der Weg ins Freie* (The road into the open), published in 1908, three years after Freud's book on joking, the Gentile protagonist Georg von Wergenthin is engaged in conversation with Jewish friends in his Viennese circle, among them the playwright Heinrich Bermann:

> Heinrich laughed. "You know the story about the Polish Jew who sat with a stranger in a railroad car, very

politely—until he realized from a remark of the other that he was a Jew, too, whereupon, with a sigh of *azoy*, he immediately put his legs up on the seat across from him?"

"Very good," said Georg.

"More than that," continued Heinrich forcefully. "Deep. Deep like so many Jewish anecdotes. They offer an insight into the tragicomedy of contemporary Judaism. They express the eternal truth that one Jew never really gets respect from another. Never. Just as little as prisoners in an enemy country show respect for one another, especially the hopeless. Envy, hatred, sometimes even admiration, in the end even love can exist between them; respect never. For all emotional relationships take place in an atmosphere of familiarity, so to speak, in which respect is stifled."

"Do you know what I think?" Georg remarked. "That you are a worse anti-Semite than most Christians I know."[6]

Both versions of this joke feature the same discourteous Galician or Polish Jew, but what Freud celebrates as creative interdependency, Heinrich deplores as self-contempt. In Schnitzler's scenario, the Jew does not tell the joke expecting to elicit a laugh; he knows that the most he can expect from the Gentile Georg is comprehension—the approbation of his "Very good." He does not tell the joke to reinforce Jewish familiarity but rather to protest the imprisoning ghetto in which it thrives. Georg, in turn, knows himself excluded by this joke about Jewish intimacy and grasps how much it owes to the anti-Semitism that calls it forth.

Freud and Schnitzler, Jewish contemporaries in Vienna, use Jewish joking to different ends. Freud delights in Jewish jokes and relays them for a general public in the same open spirit that they were told. He cheerfully pours out his evidence in a context of scientific investigation, extrapolating general principles from Jewish particulars without bothering about their provenance and ignoring that they are often antithetical to the traditions of German culture.

In contrast, Schnitzler's novel investigates the context of Freud's joking and questions its effects. Intelligent people pay attention to the social climate and don't strip naked before a frigid audience. They take into account the relation of cause and effect: Jewish joking is the product of an intricate culture, conceived in a Jewish language or idiom, drawing on Jewish memory, and responsive to shared experiences, especially of the deleterious kind. A reinforcement of collective identity, such joking necessarily calls attention to the difference between Jews and non-Jews, and even when explained, the fact that it requires explanation. The better the joke, the more it separates Jews from those it excludes. If Jews are "prisoners in an enemy country," to use Heinrich's comparison, they might do better to try to reach *der weg ins freie*, "the road to greater freedom," than to channel their humiliation into laughter. Schnitzler appreciates the humor no less than Freud, but uses it to dramatize the danger it harbors.

Just to bring the Viennese joke up to date, here is a more recent one on the relative civility of Jews and Gentiles:

> A flight to Israel in late December is about to land. "This is your captain speaking. This is the culmination of El Al

> flight 761, and we welcome you to Ben Gurion airport in Tel Aviv. Please remain seated with your seat belts fastened until the plane is at a complete standstill and the seat belt signs have been turned off. [Pause.] And to those of you who are still seated, we wish you a Merry Christmas and a Happy New Year."[7]

How do we think *this* joke would fare in mixed company? The enormous differences in culture and politics between 1908 Austrian Vienna and Cambridge, Massachusetts, a century later make it all the more curious that sympathetic listeners in both—Georg there and Samantha here—should point alike to injurious strains in this favored Jewish pastime. The laughter invoked to offset anti-Jewish hostility concedes enough of that hostility to be mistaken for the thing itself. What Jews make fun of in their own character reflects to a perilous degree what others object to. Just as inoculations can make you ill if they are too powerful, self-deprecation that is too clever, too constant, too "deep," may highlight the deformity it is trying to overcome.

Many of us experience ourselves successively or simultaneously as insiders and outsiders. That morning in the main office of Harvard's Semitic Museum—originally erected in tribute to the common origins of the three "Abrahamic" religions—telling a joke was a way of creating and enjoying camaraderie among Jews. Its unforeseen consequence was the momentary separation of us in the department along lines other than those of function (academic and nonacademic staff) and gender (males and females). Thanks to Sam's initiative, the momentary separation between Jew and Gentile was overcome. She may someday shrink it further by marrying the student she is dating. But for the moment, let us note that the discomfort to Sam is also how we know that it was a Jewish joke. You know it is vinegar when you see it separating from oil.

■ What to Expect

Jewish humor rolls cheerfully off the tongue, like *French cuisine* and *Turkish baths*. "Jewish humor is one of the wonders of the world," declares the London *Daily Telegraph*. "No other community can compete with the range and subtlety of Jewish jokes."[8] Estimates of the proportion of Jewish professionals in U.S. comedy sometimes ran as high as 80 percent. "Indeed, it is difficult to imagine what would remain of American humor in the twentieth century without its Jewish component."[9] The same has been said of Berlin in the 1920s and Russia during the seventy-five years of Bolshevik rule.

Almost as daunting as the corpus of Jewish humor is the supply of scholarship and commentary that threatens to overwhelm it. In the late 1960s BSE (before search engines), when I wrote my dissertation on the comic figure of the schlemiel as hero of modern Jewish literature, some Jewish psychoanalysts—Freud, Reik, and Martin Grotjahn—seemed the only ones apart from Yiddish literary critics who had thought deeply about the subject. Today, organizations like the Association for Applied and Therapeutic Humor, founded in 1987, and the International Society for Humor Studies, founded in 1989—there is also a (fictitious) Canadian Association for Therapeutic Humour—sit atop an ever-expanding field of scholarship interested in Jewish humor. A bibliography on a subject like the schlemiel would by now fill its own book.

This burgeoning field of study puts every general claim about Jewish humor to the test. Freud's observation, cited above, that there are few other instances of a people making fun to such a degree of its own character, has been modified by Christie Davies's comparison of Jews to Scots, who appear to have a higher proportion of self-deprecating jokes, although not in the same absolute numbers or of the same quality.[10] Elliott Oring takes exception to the assumption that Jews are "the people of the joke," pointing out that as late as 1893, the chief rabbi of London, Hermann Adler, found it necessary to defend Jews against the charge that they were a humorless people.[11] Oring argues that Jewish humor as we know it is a late invention. In turn, the conference volume *Jews and Humor,* which traces the subject from the Bible through Talmud and midrash to modern times, though with an admitted emphasis on the nineteenth and twentieth centuries, challenges Oring's contention.[12] Hillel Halkin finds the beginnings of modern Jewish humor in the Hebrew geniuses of medieval Iberia.[13] Some believe that it starts with the rise of the wedding jester, or *badkhen*.[14]

I cheerfully confess that theories about humor interest me less than the evidence they offer of folk creativity—jokes being the only surviving form of "folklore" that is not protectable by copyright. From the late eighteenth century onward, we have some record of the Jewish humor that bubbled up from below as well as whatever came from writers and intellectuals. Of all the arts, humor depends the most on its immediate context, which makes it hard to generalize about this body of wit shaped variously by different surroundings and circumstances. Getting jokes is usually the hardest stage of acculturation, and the languages in which they joked separated as much as they united Jews in modern times.

In place of a general theory, I therefore intend to offer a descriptive map of some of the centers where Jewish humor thrived and where it still prospers, drawing examples from literature and mass culture that acted on one another. These comparative instances of Jewish humor in various languages should caution against overly facile generalizations about its provenance and nature. Laughter may be universal, but we will benefit from looking at some of the market conditions governing its production and consumption.

Since books have to begin somewhere, my point of departure will be Heinrich Heine (1797–1856), whose impact on Jewish humor was stronger than anyone's until Sholem Aleichem (Sholem Rabinovich, 1859–1916), born three years after Heine died. It was Heine who set the tone for Yiddish humor magazines on the Lower East Side of New York in the first decades of the twentieth century, more than did Sholem Aleichem, who shared the language of those magazines. No image of the Jew has exerted stronger influence than Heine's of the Jewish people as a bewitched prince:

> Hund mit hündischen Gedanken,
> Kötert er die ganze Woche

Durch des Lebens Kot und Kehricht,
Gassenbuben zum Gespötte.

Aber jeden Freitagabend,
In der Dämmrungstunde, plötzlich
Weicht der Zauber, und der Hund
Wird aufs neu ein menschlich Wesen.

Mensch mit menschlichen Gefühlen,
Mit erhobnem Haupt und Herzen,
Festlich, reinlich schier gekleidet,
Tritt er in des Vaters Halle.

[As a dog, thinking doggy thoughts,
he curs it all week long
through the filth and rubbish of this world,
while street urchins mock him.

But every Friday night,
as dusk falls, suddenly
the spell is lifted, and the dog
turns, once again, into a human being.

As a man, with a man's thoughts,
head and heart proudly uplifted,
dressed festively, cleanly and neatly,
he enters his father's house.][15]

The once-sovereign Jew who is now schnorring leftovers in other people's lands appears in the poem, "Princess Sabbath," which spans the heights and depths of Jewish experience in a tragi-comic mix. Without ever naming the wizardry that has cast its evil spell on the Jews, Heine deplores what he pictures as their everyday degradation in Europe, except for the interval of dignity they assume once a week in the privacy of their homes. This representation of the Jew fallen from ancient glory and exiled from ancient homeland came from deeper in the Jewish psyche than the competing Christian and anti-Jewish image of the Wandering Ahasuerus who has been doomed for the sin of denying Christ. Many laughed with Heine at his incongruous portrait—laughed ruefully, "with lizards," as the Yiddish expression had it.

If the first chapter showcases Heine in the German sphere of Jewish humor, Sholem Aleichem follows as the central figure in the formation of Yiddish humor, drawing from intersecting streams of folk humor that converged wherever Jews lived, exploiting the wordplay of traditional sources and dialectical differences among speakers from various regions.

Once spoken by more Jews than have ever shared the same language at any time in Jewish history, Yiddish was treated by some as the mongrel of Heine's sabbath poem and charged with having stolen scraps from other languages. But the vernacular delighted in its hybridity. With little reputation to protect, Yiddish enjoyed flaunting what others considered its flaw—its mixtures and fusions—along with the tension between sabbath and weekday, or sacred and profane, that was implicit in the interplay between Hebrew and Yiddish. Yiddish, the subject of my second chapter, gave Heine's crossbreed the means to speak for itself—even to the point of mocking the culture of Heine. As if to illustrate that Yiddish allowed Jews to escape their caricature, the Yiddish and

Hebrew writer Mendele Mocher Sforim (acknowledged by Sholem Aleichem as his literary progenitor) wrote a Yiddish novel in which Heine's bewitched Jew, in the form of a mare rather than a dog, shames the reformer who tries to "civilize" her.[16] According to this version of the fable, Yiddish set the Jewish tongue free, and by allowing Jews to speak for themselves, restored them to human form.

"Now let us leave the princess and look in on the prince" is how Sholem Aleichem might have spoofed the transition from a chapter on Yiddish to one on humor in English. There was no need for Aesopian language in the lands and language of the free, because in Britain or the United States there was no political censorship of the kind that existed under the Russian czars. Discrimination against Jews abated to the point that Madison Avenue advised, "Dress British, think Yiddish." Without obscuring the differences between England and its former colony, the chapter on Jewish humor in the English language traces its phenomenal rise and spread from the Borscht Belt to the comedy clubs, from Whitechapel to the Web.

Jewish comedy must go where the Jews go, into the concentration camps of Adolf Hitler and gulags of Joseph Stalin. The witticism that stands at the heart of this book was recorded in Yiddish in the Warsaw Ghetto: "God forbid that this war should last as long as we are able to endure it." This saying pits the monomaniac obduracy of the "Final Solution" against the even greater stubbornness of Jewish survival, recognizing, however, that no such plucky stubbornness should ever have been required. By treating fascism and communism in tandem, chapter 4 shows how freely humor under oppression passed from one sphere to the other even as the humorists themselves remained trapped. Russian humor is much more abundant than German humor, but the repressive tactics of the two brutal regimes that are the targets of such jokes induced comparable and often identical humor among their Jews. One might say that modern Jews are known best through their humor and the Holocaust; while this book follows many others in celebrating the virtues of the former, it also explores correlations between it and the latter.

Finally, I approach what may prove the most lasting topic: emerging Jewish humor in the Land of Israel, where it was least expected to flourish, yet where it is by now as entrepreneurial as technology. Heine's mutt turned up early on, in unlikely form, in a novel, *Only Yesterday*, by S. Y. (Shai) Agnon (1888–1970), so far the greatest of Hebrew novelists, and there the dog runs amok—like the humor of which it forms an element. I will not trace the long and troubled path of the book's hero, Yitzhak Kumer, who arrives as a young settler in Palestine during the pioneering days, except to recall that by way of a joke, Kumer paints the words "mad dog" on the fur of a stray. Jokes have their consequences, and the dog Balak turns mad indeed and fatally bites the man who dubs him mad. That the dog also bears the name of a biblical enemy of the children of Israel invites the myriad interpretations that the book has received. According to Agnon, Heine's prince may now be restored to his homeland, but he remains in danger of self-transmogrification, of inadvertently doing damage to himself. I cite this famous episode from *Only Yesterday* merely to suggest how humor in Israel takes up the tradition into which it was born.

Yet the chapter on Israel also includes jokes that lack the angst of that tradition:

> A rabbi dies and rises to the gates of heaven. As he waits for admission, an Israeli bus driver comes up beside him. Without a second thought, the admitting angel waves the bus driver through. The rabbi cries, "Hey! How come he gets in so quickly? He's a bus driver, while I'm a rabbi!" The angel explains, "When you delivered your sermons during the prayer service, the whole congregation fell asleep. When this man drove to Tel Aviv, all his passengers were praying to God!"

Like the joke about Mrs. Rosenberg inspecting the poultry, this one, too, with a little tweaking, could be transposed to an Irish Catholic context.

■ With What Do We Eat It?

This book's inquiry into the varieties of Jewish humor in different languages and under diverse conditions hopes to advance our understanding of its various parts along with our appreciation of the whole. There is no denying that humor, the consummate insider's sport, has flourished among Jews, prompting us to ask *why* this activity should enjoy such widespread popularity. The subject begins to interest us at the point that humor is identified by others and Jews themselves as a Jewish specialty, a pursuit disproportionately associated with Jews. That this occurs only at certain points of intersection between tradition and modernity helps us arbitrate the dispute between those who want to trace its origins back to biblical times, and others who insist on its contemporaneity. Jewish humor obviously derives from Jewish civilization, but Jews became known for their humor only starting with the Enlightenment. As this book will show, it responds to conditions of Jewish life, but only where it becomes the response of choice.

This focus on Jewish humor at the point that the phrase begins to trip off the tongue accounts for what some readers may resent as the Eurocentrism of this book. Comedy and laughter are common to all cultures, and for most of Jewish history, humor was no more observably associated with Jews than with other religious or ethnic groups. In some parts of the Jewish world, this remains the case. The Ladino folktales of the Jewish trickster Joha bear a close resemblance to the Arabic ones of the Muslim trickster Juha and his Turkish counterpart Nasreddin, but recent collectors of these tales do not claim they were any more prominent among Jews than their analogous versions among other peoples of Yemen, Iran, Egypt, Turkey, or Morocco. Jewish humor in Judeo-Persian, Judeo-Arabic, and Judeo-Spanish, or Judezmo (Ladino), generated no treatises about the schlemiel or schlimazel, and no theories about parody as compensation for powerlessness. Jews laughed in Casablanca as they did in Kraków, and maybe at some of the same things, but though there are scarcely five hundred Jews left in Kraków, its bookstores still carry Polish collections of Jewish humor, whereas today's Casablanca, with more than ten times as many Jews, has no such Arabic equivalent. Jews of Arab lands appeared to have acquired no comparable *reputation* for humor.

The Yiddish expression, *mit vos est men es*? (With what does one eat this?) means something like, "Please explain to me why this matters?" or, "How does this apply?" That Jewish humor becomes prominent at a certain point does not yet address its significance or functions. How and why does it explode at the point when ghetto doors are breached, and as Jews begin mingling with fellow Europeans who also are being granted new rights and freedoms? Suppose we establish that it gains momentum among Jews who lose divine justification for their exceptionalism and now face the world stripped of the authority of the covenant in whose name they were Jews. Suppose we see its escalation in times of threat—which are nothing new in a history replete with massacres, expulsions, and inquisition, but are now experienced for the first time without the perceived protection of God in whose name Jews are being threatened. Suppose we can demonstrate that Jewish humor erupts at moments of epistemological and political crisis, and intensifies when Jews need new ways of responding to pressure. Does this mean that humor compensates them for the absent security? Does it work to their benefit or detriment? Does it become a secular expression of their identity? And what do these findings tell us about the universal significance and functions of humor?

To be sure, Oring's cautionary note about the chief rabbi of London reminds us that not everyone savored Jewish humor to the same degree. Observant Jews who kept their cultural distance from Gentile society, whether in Christian or Muslim lands, did not all take up the Jewish sport with the same enthusiasm as those who relished contradictions between the foundational idea of Jewish *chosenness* and the historical record of persecution. At the other end of the religious spectrum, young people dedicated to socialist or nationalist political action did not appreciate ridicule of their goals. "How many feminists does it take to change a lightbulb?" "That's not funny!" Ideologues do not welcome levity. Joking flourishes among those who sustain contrarieties, tolerate suspense, and perhaps even relish insecurity. Many writers featured in this book are situated—none put it better than Franz Kafka—with their posterior legs still glued to their father's Jewishness, and their waving anterior legs finding no new ground. But other Jews preferred to seek out steady, level land.

As for Jewish humor's genealogy, scholars are certainly justified in tracing its roots to its sources in the Bible and Talmud. One might locate the seeds of Jewish skepticism in Sarah's laughter when she is informed in Genesis 18:12 that she and Abraham, at their very advanced age, will conceive a child. "Therefore Sarah laughed within herself, saying, 'After I have grown old shall I have pleasure, my lord being old also?'" Joking frequently exposes unauthorized truths, and Sarah's trust in biological probability over divine prophecy is an early example of the cognitive independence that Judaism encourages. Biblical challengers to authority often outdid even the boldest of moderns in daring, and the Talmudic record of disputation supplies incontrovertible proof that Abraham and Job invited emulation on the part of generations of rabbis. Yet the Bible confirms that Sarah *did* bear Isaac, and duly named her son *Yitzhak*, signifying a laughter of joy more than cynicism; Abraham's challenge to God over His intention of destroying Sodom is finally quashed by the wickedness of that condemned city. In each case, the Bible's claim of divine authorship guarantees the predominance of the Lord's point of view. Modern humorists, in contrast, challenge authority without conceding its supreme authority.

Similarly, while Jewish tradition offers occasions of merriment and templates for humor, these are part of an ultimately, if not at all times, well-ordered universe. Jews everywhere celebrated the feast of Purim that recorded the improbable political victory of their ancestors Esther and Mordecai over their archenemy Haman in Persia. On that day of merry-making, the Talmud encourages drinking to the point that one can no longer distinguish "cursed be Haman" from "blessed be Mordecai." Some communities of eastern Europe got into the spirit of inversion by appointing a Purim rabbi to upend homiletics for a day. But in the 1930s, as we will see, a Yiddish writer forging his own rendition of the Purim story felt it necessary to add a jilted lover and failed assassin to the cast of characters to represent the disastrous realities of Jewish politics that stood in ironic contrast to the victory recorded in the Book of Esther. Rather than celebrating the exception, he reintroduced the more likely failure, reversing the reversal, recording what the Jews of Europe were actually experiencing in his time.

Modern Yiddish "proverbs" did the same with the liturgy: "Thou hast chosen us from among the nations—why did you have to pick on the Jews?" "God will provide—if only He would provide until He provides." "Pray to the Lord—and talk to the wall." Whereas religion reinforced God's promise, modern humor questions His constancy. True, modern scholarship has found commonalities in the language play of the midrash and Marx Brothers, and some of this material will be alluded to in the following chapters. But it was only in the modern period that humor became the *aim* of such entertainment as opposed to a delightful by-product of otherwise-earnest interpretation.

All this is to say that this book explores Jewish humor at the point that it becomes a modern phenomenon. A creation of the Jewish people, drawing on its texts and habits of mind as well as heart, reflecting its historical development and interaction with surrounding cultures, it emerges from Baruch Spinoza's mid-seventeenth-century denial of any functional reciprocity between the divine and human spheres, thus undercutting the philosophical basis of the covenant without dissolving the community formed by its demands. The ensuing rifts between the religious and agnostics, elites and masses, and especially warring impulses of loyalty and restiveness within individual Jews and their communities generates the humor that is this book's subject. Jews who found cognitive security in tradition or revolution may not have needed humor to reconcile their contrarieties, but they became the unwitting butt of the conflicted Jews who did.

An association with humor would seem to have benefited Jews, since physiologists nowadays confirm the advantages of joking, long since touted by philosophers:

> [Laughing] lowers blood pressure, reduces stress hormones, increases muscle flexion, and boosts immune func-

> tion by raising levels of infection-fighting T-cells, disease-fighting proteins called Gamma-interferon and B-cells, which produce disease-destroying antibodies. Laughter also triggers the release of endorphins, the body's natural painkillers, and produces a general sense of well-being.[17]

A popular Web site lists among the benefits of laughter everything from the relief of physical tension and prevention of heart disease to strengthened friendships and the promotion of group bonding.[18] Sholem Aleichem was fond of saying, "Laughter is good for you. Doctors prescribe laughter."[19] Now that its therapeutic value is being scientifically confirmed, why would anyone question the merits of joking?

Yet I am obliged to ask whether an excess of laughter might exacerbate the tensions it is meant to alleviate. Can a surfeit of comedy be unhealthy? Is there a point at which too much joking could cause someone harm? In his biography of Lenny Bruce, Albert Goldman describes a fellow comedian engaging in what Germans call *Todlachen*—making people helpless with laughter so that they beg him to stop. "When he sees you're on the ropes, going down, he works twice as hard to kill you. Zooms in close to your face, locks onto the rhythms of your body, lasers and razors you till finally you tear yourself away."[20] The ostensible provider of psychic relief appears to have become an instrument of torture. As it happens, Sholem Aleichem uses the quoted tagline, "Doctors prescribe laughter," at the end of a story that takes its hero beyond comedy into madness. Speaking as the professed comic writer, he asks the readers' pardon for having been unable to rescue the humor from its end in tragedy. The late rabbi Joshua Schmidman, who had considered becoming a stand-up comic but found himself officiating instead at a great many funerals, was fond of reminding his congregation that Judaism considered dying only a minhag, not a mitzvah. He might have said the same about joking: it is only a custom, not a religious imperative, and it is a custom that may be revved up into overkill.

■ Caveat Emptor

I was once addressing an academic audience, and caught off guard by a request to tell them my favorite Yiddish joke, could only come up with a quip attributed to the Zionist activist Shmaryahu Levin: *di yidn zenen a kleyn folk, nor paskudne*, "Jews are a small people, but rotten." A deadly silence fell, and my discomfort was so great I felt obliged to try to explain: "The expected reversal introduced by 'but' is supposed to be followed by a mitigating quality to compensate the Jews for their 'smallness.' Instead, it damns them for their nastiness," or words to that effect. All the while, I was thinking, How fortunate the audience that doesn't understand Levin's sally! Anyone who lives at the heart of the Jewish community—of any community—and is fighting an uphill battle for what they think is in its best interest would appreciate the frustrations that triggered this epigram. Levin (1867–1935) might happily have traded in the witticism for a stretch of Jewish history calmer than the one he had to navigate.

An analogous moment of bitter intimacy occurs in the wondrous story "Gedali" by the Russian Jewish writer Isaac Babel (1894–1940). The tale is based on Babel's own experiences as a Soviet propagandist for the Bolshevik revolution. His narrator, Lyutov, is accompanying the Red Army as it fights its way into Poland, harassing (to put it mildly) the Jews in the small towns it occupies. One Friday evening, Lyutov is engaged in a conversation with a Jewish shopkeeper, Gedali, who cannot reconcile the revolution's stated intentions with the barbarous actions of its enforcers. The old Jew complains, "The International, comrade, one does not know what to eat it with." "One eats it with gunpowder," I replied to the old man, "And seasons it with the finest blood."[21]

Gedali's Yiddish expression, mit vos est men es, translated in the Russian text, conveys how much understanding still exists between these two politically divided Yiddish speakers, and also between the author, Babel, and the native language and culture that he is suppressing. Lyutov's reply is as brutal as the actions of the Cossack soldiers. Of all those who justified Bolshevism, no one ever assumed as much moral blame for it as this Jewish writer from the Odessan Jewish heartland, who did finally season it with the finest blood—his own. Babel *exaggerated* his complicity with evil in order to exploit for irony the paradoxes of a Yiddish-speaking Jew (himself) defending the violence of Cossacks to a fellow Jew with whom he then welcomes in the sabbath.

My discussion of humor, which includes all manner of comedy, satire, and irony commensurate with the ironies of Jewish experience, goes well beyond light entertainment and what some consider funny. It is therefore not surprising that in the following chapters, some of the strongest warnings against the excesses of humor come from its finest practitioners—Kafka, Sholem Aleichem, Babel, and Philip Roth—which of course did not prevent them from continuing the practice. If there were an Olympics for irony, *Hatikvah* (The Hope), might be the most played national anthem in the world. The Zionist leader Ze'ev Jabotinsky is reputed to have said of it, "Don't count on me to stand still during the singing of the national anthem if at the same moment I feel someone picking my pocket."

When they search for universal aspects of human behavior, social scientists—many of them Jews—sometimes underplay the distinctions among cultures. But as long as Jewish experience remains distinctive, so, too, will its impulse for laughter. This book demonstrates how the benefits of Jewish humor are reaped from the paradoxes of Jewish life, so that Jewish humor at its best carries the scars of the convulsions that brought it into being.

Which might have remained an insular problem were it not for the fact that by now, much of the United States is almost as addicted to joking as are the Jews. News programs regularly end with comic segments, as though the reporters were charged to leave 'em laughing. We are told that most young people take their news straight—straight from the comedians. When did news get to be an excuse for comedy? Or rather, when did Americans begin to deal with the news by laughing at its absurdities and their own attempts to solve the problems of the world?

Laughter may be the best medicine, but conscientious doctors also warn against overdose.

German Lebensraum

"[Do] you believe that one's inner nature is completely altered by baptism? Do you believe that one can change lice into fleas by pouring water on them?"

"I don't believe it."

"I don't, either, and for me it is a sight as melancholy as it is ridiculous. . . . I have seen on the street in Berlin old daughters of Israel wearing long crosses at their throats, crosses that were longer than their noses and reached to their navels; in their hands they held a Protestant hymn book, and they spoke of the splendid sermon they had just heard in Trinity Church. . . . Even more repellent to me was the sight of dirty bearded Jews who came out of their Polish cloaca in order to be solicited for heaven by the Conversion Society in Berlin, and preached Christianity in their mumbling dialect and stank so horribly. It would in any case be desirable if one were to baptize that sort of Polish lice-folk not with ordinary water but with eau de Cologne."

"In the house of the hanged," I interrupted him, "one does not talk about ropes, my dear doctor."

—Heinrich Heine, *Ludwig Börne: A Memorial*

At the dawn of the twentieth century, when Theodor Herzl drew up his vision for the Jewish future in Palestine, he included a withering portrait of the European Jews he was hoping to transform. His 1902 novel, *Altneuland* (Old-new land), features Viennese Jews afraid to speak freely in front of their Christian servants and young professionals with no practical prospects of employment or matrimony. In the novel, a Dr. Friedrich Loewenberg, an "educated, desperate young man," attends a lavish engagement party—really a disguised business merger between the families of a well-born male and the female whom Loewenberg himself is hoping to marry. For Herzl, the scene demonstrates why Jews need a home in Palestine even more urgently than Palestine, the ancient Jewish homeland, needs the return of its Jews.

The dinner guests whom Herzl mocks include a financial speculator, several industrialists, a representative of Baron Goldstein (read Rothschild), and Messrs. Gruen and Blau, the "two wittiest men in Vienna." "Why so late, Mr. Gruen?" asks the hostess. "Because I could come no later."[1] Returning insult for courtesy, the entertainers Gruen and Blau are evidently much in demand: "no reception, no wedding, no betrothal party or anything else comes off without them." Herzl shows us a Jewish society that fearing the Gentiles, cultivates an aggressive humor whose malice is directed chiefly against its own kind. Thus, when another invited guest, Rabbi Weiss from a provincial town in Moravia, ventures some shy remarks about the new movement to resurrect a Jewish homeland in Palestine, the two wits lead the charge in merriment. Gruen volunteers to be Palestine's new ambassador to Vienna. Blau protests that too many Jews would be competing for that post. In any case, Goldstein should be the appointed king of the Jewish land, rewarding public benefactors with the Order of the Fleishik Sword—an allusion to the kosher laws that require separate cutlery for dairy and meat.

Herzl was a popular dramatist before he became a political leader, and here he appropriates for his own satiric purposes the barbs that were already greeting his Zionist idea. But in the latter part of the novel, where he sketches his vision of the new society in Palestine, he turns the tables on Gruen and Blau. The two men, having come to visit the land whose emergence they once ridiculed, are being shown around by Friedrich, who is now their host.

> Gruen, the jester, was holding forth. "Well, Dr. Loewenberg, and how do you like it here? What! You find no words! Perhaps you think there are too many Jews here!"
>
> Laughter. "I am frank to say," remarked Friedrich slowly, "that you are the first person to have made me think so."
>
> "Ha! Ha! Ha! Very good!" laughed [one of the visiting Viennese]. The others joined in the merriment. Only then did Friedrich realize that his remark had been construed as one of the rude wisecracks common in this set.[2]

Friedrich, that is, has been witty only unintentionally. In harmony with himself, he no longer has need of double meanings. Irony is for those who accept the threatening conditions in which they choose to live, whereas the new society tackles imperfection instead of joking about it. Where Jews are free to realize their ambitions to the limits of their abilities, the wit of Gruen and Blau is stale and superfluous.

How very different from Herzl's disparagement of self-directed Jewish wit is the praise of its restorative value by his Viennese contemporary Freud! The founder of psychoanalysis was a great lover of Jewish joking, and for many years collected material for the study that would appear in 1905 as *Jokes and Their Relation to the Unconscious*. He appreciated one-liners: "A wife is like an umbrella; sooner or later one takes a cab." He was fond of wordplay: old people fall into "anecdotage"; the Christmas season kicks off the "alcoholidays." He especially favored Jewish jokes in which matchmakers, rabbis, and sophisticated beggars, or schnorrers, upend our expectations of them:

> The young man was most disagreeably surprised when the proposed bride was introduced to him, and drew aside the *shadkhen*—the marriage broker—to whisper his objections: "Why have you brought me here?" he asked reproachfully. "She's ugly and old, she squints, and has bad teeth . . ." "You needn't lower your voice," interrupted the broker, "she's deaf as well."

> Two Jews meet in a railway carriage at a station in Galicia. "Where are you going?" asks one. "To Cracow," replied the other. "What a liar you are!" objects the first. "If you say you're going to Cracow, you want me to believe you're going to Lemberg. But I know that in fact you're going to Cracow. So why are you lying to me?"

> A schnorrer, who was allowed as a guest into the same house every Sabbath, appeared one day in the company of an unknown young man who was about to sit down at the table. "Who is this?" asked the householder. "He's my new son-in-law," the schnorrer replied. "I've promised him his board for the first year."[3]

In the first joke, expecting the shadkhen to parry the young man's objections, we are surprised that he reinforces them instead. In the second, convolution, which normally serves to obscure the truth, ends up confirming it. In the third, the beggar assumes the host's prerogative, manifesting largesse at the expense of his benefactor. Reversal, displacement, and turning the tables are the wellsprings of a tradition that mocks the contradictions of Jewish experience—the gap between accommodation to foreign powers and promise of divine election. Although many religions acknowledge a tension between the tenets and confutations of their faith, few have had to balance such high national hopes against such a poor political record. Jewish humor at its best interprets the incongruities of the Jewish condition.

But I am doing what Freud does not. Though he draws heavily on the humor of his native Jewish culture, he extrapolates from it only such findings as are presumably universal. He is interested in the relation of joking to other psychological phenomena, not in relation to Jews. "[We] do not insist upon a patent of nobility from our examples," he writes. "We make no inquiries about their origin but only about their efficiency—whether they are capable of making us laugh and whether they deserve our theoretical interest. And both these two requirements are best fulfilled precisely by Jewish jokes."[4]

One can't help musing on the analyst's reluctance to comment on the Jewishness of the Jewish material he discusses. Take a phrase like "patent of nobility"—transposed from the Yiddish *yikhes-briv*, a hybrid Hebrew-Yiddish term for pedigree. The irony implicit in Freud's use of the term, which follows a joke about Jews' aversion to bathing, derives from the distinction between Jewish and Christian-European concepts of nobility, with each side looking down on the standards of the other. Freud's obvious pride in the claim of Jews to primogeniture as well as cultural and ethical advantages over their Christian overlords belies the scientist's claim to be transcending parochialism.

Only once in this book does Freud indulge in some speculation about the specifically Jewish affinity for humor. He does so during a discussion of tendentious jokes, "when the intended rebellious criticism is directed against the subject himself, or, to put it more cautiously, against someone in whom the subject has a share—a collective person, that is (the subject's own nation, for instance)." In other words, Freud makes a distinction between jokes directed by Jews at Jews and jokes directed at Jews by foreigners—not because the former are any kinder, but instead because Jews know the connection between their own faults and virtues. "Incidentally," he concludes this part of the exploration with a sentiment already cited in the introduction, "I do not know whether there are many other instances of a people making fun to such a degree of its own character."[5] The offhand quality of this observation has not prevented it from becoming the most quoted sentence in Freud's book, perhaps because others have realized better than the author how much it says about the Jewish condition.

Herzl and Freud, otherwise so alike in their German Jewish ambience and restless intelligence, reached opposite conclusions about Jewish humor. Both recognized its connection to anti-Jewish hostility, but Freud admired what Herzl—like Schnitzler in *Der Weg ins Freie*—feared. Freud put up with anti-Semitism in much the same way that he accepted civilization *with* its discontents (to paraphrase the title of one of his most famous works).[6] He therefore welcomed joking as a compensatory pleasure—the expressive venting of people who lived under the double weight of their own disciplining heritage and the collective responsibility to behave well among the nations. Herzl, in contrast, wanted to alleviate anti-Semitism for the betterment of Europe as well as the Jews.

Which of the two thinkers do we consider the greater "realist"? Which the greater optimist? Which the greater healer? At issue here is the degree to which the two men's approval of Jewish wit was proportional to their respective plans, if any, for Jewish rescue.

■ Heine

The fountainhead and genius of German Jewish humor was neither Herzl nor Freud but rather Heine, who was also the most controversial figure in modern German literature.[7] Coming of age at a moment when Jews were being admitted to German society, Heine knew he had something fresh to introduce into the high culture of Johann Wolfgang von Goethe and Friedrich von Schiller—namely, a literature less focused than theirs on achieving comprehensive truth and classical perfection, and thus truer to the volatile realities of the day. Had his precursors not set a high bar for German literature, he might not have held himself to a standard of honesty and self-exposure that was bold to the point of recklessness. But whatever the motivation, no Jewish writer ever took more aggressive risks.

Born in Düsseldorf, then under French rule, in 1797, Heine published his first book of poems in 1821. Though he studied law and philosophy, he was a natural poet, pushing the form to the limits of lyrical, political, and critical expression. His writing drew on warring elements in his nature: romantic longing versus analytic skepticism, socialist sympathies tempered by monarchist preferences, and a love of the German language and homeland that endured a quarter century's residence in France. In his lyrics, Heine proved that he could "do" perfection; over seventy-five composers, including Franz Peter Schubert, Felix Mendelssohn, Robert Schumann, Franz Liszt, and Richard Wagner, set his poems to music. Sharing a widespread contemporary attraction to folk poetry, Heine achieved some of its effects of "artlessness" in his art. But he was just as keen to register imperfections—in politics, human nature, and himself. Heine's trustiest biographer, Jeffrey L. Sammons, advises extreme caution in describing both who Heine was and who Heine thought he was, and the avalanche of arguments over his legacy renders foolish any attempt to provide a definitive characterization of the man and his career.

Controversy over the memorialization of Heine in Germany has kept pace with the controversy over his work. This monument in Düsseldorf's Swan Market by the sculptor Bert Gerresheim situates an enlarged replica of the author's death mask in a landscape of ruin. The prominence of the nose in this magnified form disturbed some viewers as a reminder of the anti-Semitic trope of the Jewish nose—a trope exploited for humor by Heine himself.

Heine's conversion to Christianity, for example—an act that was fairly common among his Jewish contemporaries—acquired notoriety only because he cast himself as at once a renegade Jew and phony Christian. He called his conversion an *Entréebillet zur europäischen Kultur*—a jibe that had many teeth. By using the French term for "ticket of admission," he implied that the German language had to pay its own ticket of admission into European culture, just as the Jew paid through baptism for his. In addition, the commercial terminology mocks both conversion as a religious experience and the person who submits to it, not to mention others as well. Christians are ridiculed for accepting inauthentic converts, Jews for trading their culture for one that despises theirs, and enlightened Europeans for exposing the bias at the heart of their liberal affectations by requiring the credential of Christian baptism that they otherwise pretended to spurn. In a single breath, Heine thus damns all parties to the dishonest bargain and himself most of all, since he knew that the teaching post he hoped to gain by his conversion had not come through. Like Samson among the Philistines, he pulls down the pillars of the civilization that had seduced him, accepting—or rather seeking—his own punishment along with that of his seducers.

When I studied eighteenth- and nineteenth-century European literature in college, Heine's lyric "Ein Fichtenbaum steht einsam" was presented as the epitome of Romantic longing. It depicts a pine tree standing lonely on a northern height, slumbering under its cover of snow and ice, and dreaming of a palm tree, in the East, that mourns lonely and silent on a blazing cliff.

> Ein Fichtenbaum steht einsam
> Im Norden auf kahler Höh.
> Ihn schläfert; mit weisser Decke
> Umhüllen ihn Eis und Schnee.
>
> Er träumt von einer Palme,
> Die, fern im Morgenland,

Einsam und schweigend trauert
Auf brennender Felsenwand.[8]

[There stands a lonely pine-tree
In the north, on a barren height;
He sleeps while the ice and snow flakes
Swathe him in folds of white.

He dreameth of a palm-tree
Far in the sunrise-land,
Lonely and silent longing
On her burning bank of sand.][9]

Male pine and female palm, each solitary, majestic, and destined to yearn for what can never be joined, are coupled in the harmonious medium of a lied—German for poem and song—that forges their conciliation across the gap between the two stanzas. The accord of the words supplants the rupture of feeling.

This is the kind of poetry at which Heine excelled, but it was not the only kind. Another way of expressing the same *Zerrissenheit*—the condition of being torn apart—was through wit. This, too, yokes opposites, although instead of harmonizing the disjunction, wit accentuates it by means of verbal surprise. In fact, Heine was superb at puncturing the very ideals of love and beauty that he elsewhere upheld. Although by no means the only practitioner of the aggressive wit that came to be known as *Judenwitz* (a form also practiced by non-Jews), he became its master.

If I were teaching European Romanticism today, I might tweak the syllabus to include, alongside "Ein Fichtenbaum," one of Heine's comic takes on the Romantic poet (that is, himself) who wrote it. "The Baths of Lucca," one of his four so-called travel pictures, has the added advantage of being a send-up of Jews. The parody begins with the genre. Modeling himself on then-popular accounts of which the best known was Goethe's *Travels in Italy*, Heine confesses that "there's nothing more boring on this earth than to have to read the description of an Italian journey—except maybe to have to write one—and the writer can only make it halfway bearable by speaking as little as possible of Italy itself."[10] Accordingly, the Tuscan resort town of Lucca serves Heine merely as the setting for an encounter among displaced German Jews who have come to take the baths.

The plot of this travelogue is minimal. The implied author, identified as Heine, doctor of laws, drops in on Lady Matilda, whom he had previously known in London. The narrator recognizes a second visitor as the converted Jewish Hamburg banker Christian Gumpel, now the Marquis Christoforo di Gumpelino, who pronounces himself madly in love with Matilda's countrywoman, Lady Julie Maxfield. To while away the time, the two prospective suitors set out to visit Gumpelino's local Italian lady friends. Huffing and puffing through the picturesque hills of Lucca, they encounter Gumpel's valet, also recognizable to the author as Old Hirsch, his former Hamburg lottery agent. While the author and Gumpelino pay an extended visit to the Italian courtesans, the servant is dispatched to arrange an evening rendezvous for his master with Maxfield. The erotic adventure subsequently falls through, and the work concludes with an improbable discussion of poetry in which the "author" makes merciless fun of August von Platen (1796–1835), a fellow poet in real life. This part of the work damaged Heine's reputation harder than it did von Platen's.

In the sunny opening chapters of "The Baths of Lucca," the main target of ridicule is Gumpelino, the Jewish convert to Catholicism and newly minted marquis. Matilda reveals her prejudice against this man when she tells Dr. Heine not to be put off by his nose, which then becomes the focus of a *shpritz* (a "spray" or "squirt," as in a squirt of flavor into a soda, later a Jewish American term for an extended comic riff):

> Matilda's warning not to knock against the nose of the man was sufficiently well-founded, a little more length and he'd have surely poked my eye out with it. I don't want to say anything bad about that nose; quite the contrary, it was of the noblest form, and in a sense it's what gave my friend the right to add a Marquis' title to his name. For one could tell from his nose that he came from noble stock, that he descended from an ancient international family with which even our Lord God established nuptial ties without fear of rendering Himself déclassé.[11] This family has indeed come down in the world a notch or two since then, so that, ever since Charlemagne's day, most are compelled to earn their living by peddling old trousers and Hamburg lottery tickets, albeit without in the least letting up on their pride of ancestry or ever abandoning hope of recuperating their old holdings, or at least receiving adequate compensation for emigration,

> if ever their old legitimate Sovereign fulfills his promise of restoration, a promise by which He's already led them around by the nose for two thousand years. Did their noses perhaps grow so long from being so long led around by the nose? Or are these long noses a kind of uniform whereby Jehovah, the King of Kings, might recognize His old yeomen of the guard even if they deserted the ranks? The Marquis Gumpelino was just such a deserter, but he still wore his uniform, and it was ever so brilliant, adorned with little crosses and stars and rubies, a red coat of arms in miniature and plenty of other decorations, too.[12]

Ah, that nose. Where Matilda mocks Gumpel's protuberance, the narrator, speaking as a proper Protestant and without betraying his Jewish origins, beats her at her own game by mocking the bloodline that as a Christian, she shares. Religion is treated as a social commodity. Judaism gets the brunt of the ridicule, but the credulous Jewish tribe comes off more appealingly than does the Jew who believes he is trading up by discarding it. Like Freud in the passage quoted earlier, Heine draws attention to the "noble stock"—ancient and related to God—that he simultaneously puts down, with the nose as the ambiguous marker of both superiority and slavish servitude. Underlying this ambiguity is the reality of Europe, some of whose autocrats were intent on preventing the "progress" of their restive subjects. In such changeable times, did Jews prove their mettle by staying Jewish or by leaving their Jewishness behind?

The dramatic construction of this work assigns to Matilda the meaner prejudice and to the Heine stand-in a loftier skepticism—one that also distinguishes him from Gumpelino's wholehearted devotion to his new religion and position. Both men are converts, but Gumpelino is *sincere*—in his adopted Catholicism, acquired romanticism, and passion for a married woman. An all-purpose worshipper, an enthusiast of nature, he declares Heine a torn man, a torn soul, "a Byron, so to speak." But the Byronic author revels in the discordances of his life. "Whosoever claims that his heart is still whole merely acknowledges that he has a prosaic . . . heart." Once upon a time the world was whole, but since then the world itself has been ripped in two. "[The] wretched worldwide tear of our time runs right through my heart, and for that very reason I know that the great gods have shown mercy and deemed me worthy of a poet's martyrdom."[13] The divided being personifies the spirit of the times, and none more so than the Jew, living in one place while belonging to another, claiming election and experiencing subjection, and in Heine's case, raised in one religious tradition and acculturating to another without wholly letting go of the first.

It is worth recalling that Heine's near-contemporary Nahman of Bratslav (1772–1810), the Hasidic master from western Ukraine whom I will discuss in the next chapter, is credited with having said *Es iz nito keyn gantsere zakh vi a tsebrokhn harts*, "there is nothing as whole as a broken heart." (A folk tradition added, "a broken *Jewish* heart.") The novelty of these insights lay in their elevation of rupture into the defining condition of modern people. The Bible describes how after Moses shattered the first tablets of the law, he returned for a new, unbroken set, thereby upholding the ideal of moral perfection while acknowledging the difficulty of attaining it. For their part, Nahman and Heine accept fracture—the former in metaphysical and the latter in earthly terms. Yearning is Nahman's expression of faith in the ultimate, messianic reunion beyond the world as we know it. Heine treats his yearning as a comic relic, as if the human were longing for its absent tail.

Another comically bifurcated modern is Gumpelino's valet, Old Hirsch, the third Jew of "The Baths of Lucca," who never converts to Catholicism like Gumpelino or to Protestantism like Heine, but instead accepts the position of servant as the price of remaining the Jew he is. As he approaches from the distance, the narrator tells us,

> I recognized someone whom I'd have sooner expected to meet on Mount Sinai than on the Apennines, and that was none other than Old Hirsch, sometime resident in Hamburg, a man who had not only made his mark as an incorruptible lottery collector but who was likewise so knowledgeable about foot-corns and jewels that he could not only distinguish between the two but also skillfully excise the former and precisely appraise the latter.[14]

On drawing closer, Hirsch hopes that the author will still recognize him even though his name is now . . . Hyazinth. Gumpelino is outraged at his servant's revelation of their common past, but Hirsch-Hyazinth compulsively blurts out what his master has tried to conceal. The entire passage is a palimpsest of the newly minted European superimposed on the ghetto Jew—a figure who has adapted to his new condition and name without shedding his old skin. Heine, who elsewhere pits Hebraism against Hellenism, here forges a character in whom Jew and Greek are improbably combined. No wonder this man should be a connoisseur at once of bunions and gems, the irritants and adornments of living. Hyazinth later boasts about the money he has saved by retaining his initial when he changed his name—a little joke at the expense of the author, who had presumably enjoyed a similar economy when he exchanged Harry for Heinrich, but who turned out to be both less competent and less well adjusted.

He is also not as funny. Though Heine declares himself the master poet of *Zerrissenheit*, he assigns to his creation Hirsch-Hyazinth the wittiest wordplays, including one analyzed to death by Freud—"I sat next to Salomon Rothschild, and he treated me as his equal, altogether *famillionairely*."[15] The servant describes his master Gumpelino kneeling in adoration every evening for a full two hours before the "*pri*madonna with the Christ child"—a painting that cost him six hundred silver coins. He also yearns for "Hamburg with its apes and excellent humans and *Papagoyim*." *Papageien*, German for parrots, are here punned into a species of humans who mimic the Gentiles.[16] Do these wordplays highlight the imperfect attempts of people to be other than they are or repair a torn world through comically improbable fusions?

Since this work is also a species of bourgeois comedy, servant gets the better of master. Gumpelino is an overreacher: his nose is too long, and his ambitions are beyond his talents. He imagines himself as Romeo, casting his love for "Julie" in Shakespearean verse; just as friar and nurse mismanage the nuptials in William Shakespeare's tragedy, Gumpelino's servant, Hyazinth, gives "magical" salts to the pining lover just minutes before a note arrives from Maxfield saying that she *can* see him that night after all. The honeypot yields to the chamber pot as Gumpelino is literally flushed out in a cruel scatological jest.

Were this a film by Sacha Baron Cohen or Larry David—two contemporary comics who resort to bathroom humor—the purgation of Gumpel during the night of intended bliss would have constituted its climax. But Heine aims higher. More than Gumpelino's pretensions, at stake for Heine is the reputation of poetry—the supreme form of human expression, quintessence of a nation's achievement, and trustiest manifestation of the zeitgeist. To the ideal of poetry, Heine transfers the respect that he denies to formal religion, declaring it sinful to cheapen the sublime art and heretical to use it to evil ends. Gumpelino spends his night of agony reading *Poems of Count August von Platen*, a book "scented with that curious perfume not in the least related to eau de cologne, and perhaps to be ascribed to the fact that the Marquis had spent the whole night reading it." Shifting the target of his satire from the consumer to the producer of smelly art, Heine in the last third of the work drops the travelogue frame in order to fatten von Platen up "as the Iroquois do with the captives they look forward to feeding on at a future festivity."[17]

Many critics, then and since, have pounced on Heine for his ridicule of von Platen, which the Oxford literary scholar Sigmund Prawer calls "a disgraceful performance."[18] Prawer was so distressed that he omitted any discussion of the offensive passages in his eight-hundred-page book *Heine's Jewish*

Comedy. With somewhat-greater latitude, the German literary critic Hans Mayer, who was both a Jew and homosexual, suggests that in this contest between two social "outsiders," Heine exposed anxieties about his own manhood as well as von Platen's.[19] All this is just to say that the affront of the satire does not appear to have dulled with time. Heine had no use for the forced metrics of von Platen's verse or his veiled, mawkish way of treating his homosexuality. He taunts von Platen's alleged pedophilia (which he has in common with Nero) and practices that have him listening "*a posteriori* to the intimate doings of his enemies." Von Platen's chief offense, however, was to have written a play, *The Romantic Oedipus*, which "outed" Heine as a former Jew. This clumsy exposure is what earned Heine's retaliatory exposure of von Platen as a beggar pretending to be an aristocrat, a dishonest romancer, an inferior versifier, and a sexual deviant:

> Through a few slight modifications in the play's storyline he might . . . have made better use of Oedipus, the key protagonist of his comedy. Instead of having him kill his father Laius and marry his mother Jocasta, he should, quite the contrary, have had Oedipus kill his mother and marry his father.

Clearly, von Platen had overreached in choosing *his* target.

Prawer's delicacy aside, it is worth inquiring why a work that starts out in sunny comedy should end in an aggression so dark that Heine had to assure his readers: "It's all just a joke."[20] Heine did not need to be told that his work violated standards of comedy; no, this must have been the ending he required. There was, indeed, plenty to dislike in von Platen, a lesser talent who had landed a private royal bequest and publication by Cotta, Goethe's publisher—two honors that Heine himself craved. Yet that alone would scarcely have triggered this "excessive and still very, very witty diatribe."[21] Nor would Heine, who flaunted his Byronic character, have protested von Platen's association of Jews with "romantics"—people who were not whole in the classical sense, but instead fatally split in their natures. Mayer's explanation of Heine's outsider complex seems less direct and more contrived than Heine's work itself. What hurt was the self-inflicted wound—the conversion that would forever expose him to charges of inauthenticity, with all its attendant vices: hypocrisy, cowardice, and disloyalty. Von Platen's attempt to hide his own truer, "feminine" nature is compared by Heine to the ostrich, "who believes himself hidden when he's stuck his head in the sand, so that only the bum remains visible." Von Platen might one day raise his head from the sand and speak as a proud homosexual, while the shame of Heine's conversion could never be erased. In short, von Platen is there to remind Heine that there was no way of cutting off the nose without spiting the race.

As opposed to all the pretenders—Gumpelino, Heine, and von Platen—the moral high ground of the satire is entrusted to the Jew who did not undergo baptism: Hirsch-Hyazinth, the lottery collector. Here is a Jew who had stayed honorable in a corrupting business—unlike the author, who had violated his own standards of integrity. And to whom does Hirsch-Hyazinth ascribe the moral high ground? While mocking all religions—Catholicism smells of incense, Protestantism is harmless and ineffectual, the old Jewish faith brings nothing but hard luck, and Reform Judaism is too good for the common man—he grants a measure of approval to a poor but contented ghetto Jew, Moses Little Lump, whose sabbath compensates for the woes of the week, and whose history of suffering makes him appreciate the value of life.

> [The] man is happy, he need not torment himself with self-cultivation, he sits content in his religion and his green dressing gown like Diogenes in his barrel, he takes pleasure in the light of his candelabrum which he himself doesn't have to polish—and I tell you, even if the candelabrum burns a bit dimly and the hired hand who's supposed to keep it spotless isn't at hand, and Rothschild the Great happened by at that very moment with all his agents, wholesalers, and *chefs de comptoir*, with the aid of which he conquers the world, and Rothschild said, "Moses Lump, you may have a single wish, whatever you want, it shall be done," . . . I'm quite sure Moses Lump would promptly reply, "Polish my candelabrum!" and Rothschild the Great would reply in wonderment, "If I wasn't Rothschild, I'd want to be a Little Lump like this!"[22]

This ironic vision of Rothschild bending to the whims of a little Jew became a staple of Jewish comedy. It was at the opposite remove from German high culture where von Platen and Heine competed for supremacy. And it was a fantasy, designed to mitigate the actual growing rifts between rich and poor within Jewish communities, and demonstrating Jewish unity against the double threat of anti-Jewish aggression and assimilation. Yiddish referred to this unifying intra-Jewish quality as *dos pintele yid*, "the little marker of the Jew," signifying the quintessence of Jewishness that remains when all else may have been lost. (The term was itself a bit of a joke, punning on the dot beneath the *yud*, the smallest letter in the Hebrew alphabet.)

Heine's comedy thus highlights the diminutive aspect of those who preserve their innocence. In the reverse hierarchy of moral standing, Hirsch-Hyazinth defers to Little Lump, Dr. Heine to Hirsch-Hyazinth, and Rothschild to them all—and the Gentiles to Rothschild. Correspondingly, however, Heine, the one furthest from the ghetto, is the freest to speak his mind. Only the baptized Dr. Heine can really attack the anti-Jew, since Jews within the fold, even one as loose-tongued as Hirsch, must stay under the cover of comedy, preemptively cautious, fearing collective as well as personal reprisal. Indeed, it is at the point where Heine's comedy lurches out of control, where he breaches the boundaries of good taste and humor itself, that we see the full gain of the freedoms he flaunted along with the full cost.

■ German Jews who converted or stood close to conversion—in a progression that extended from Heine's contemporary Ludwig Börne (1786–1837) to the satirist Karl Kraus (1874–1936)—produced some of the most aggressive comedy in Europe. Accused of "self-hatred" because of their delight in assailing Jews, they were equally hard on Gentiles. As one can see in the epigraph to this chapter, where the author reminds Börne, his fellow convert, that "one does not talk of ropes in the house of the hanged," Heine leaves ambiguous whether the metaphoric hanging (read: conversion) was by the deceased's own hand or another's—whether, that is, the Jews had more to fear from Gentiles than from their own impulse of surrender. The Enlightenment abandoned the dreadful measures used by the Inquisition to deal with suspected aliens and backsliders, but still there remained something toxic in the encounter between Jewish and German cultures—something that was conspicuous in the comedy from early on. At the same time, comedy's predilection for inversion and incongruity was richly served by a society that enticed Jews into conversions that it necessarily distrusted, and Jews who distrusted the society into which they were voluntarily coerced.

■ Kafka

This cultural predicament received its iconic treatment in the work of the Czech writer Franz Kafka, though by the time of his death in 1924 historical conditions were hardening in ways that made it hard to laugh at his comic turns. German was Kafka's language and formative literary tradition, but unlike with Heine, his circle of Jews in Prague sought not so much a cultural synthesis as a cultural give-and-take. Kafka, for example, became for a time a devotee of Yiddish theater, to the point of championing the language against those who considered it merely an inferior version of German. He read up on Jewish history and frequented a Jewish study group where the philosopher Martin Buber came to lecture. Multiethnic

The monument to Kafka in the former Jewish quarter of Prague is a bronze statue by Jaroslav Rona, unveiled in December 2003. According to the sculptor, it is based on a paragraph in Kafka's story "Description of a Struggle" in which the narrator leaps on another man's shoulders and urges him forward into a trot. Here, a smaller Kafka sits atop a headless, handless, and footless, but striding, giant of a man. Courtesy of Hyde Flippo.

Prague, with its built-in competition between Czech and German, was much more conducive to Jewish self-awareness than unilingual German cities or German-monopolized Vienna.

The deracinated European Jew became Kafka's special subject. One of his funniest send-ups in this vein, the story "A Report to an Academy," appeared in 1917 in the Zionist periodical that Buber edited, demonstratively called *Der Jude* (The Jew).[23] Talking animals have made people laugh since before Aristophanes, and in this "report" one of Charles Darwin's subjects returns the compliment of his theory by describing how the ape turned human.

Five years after his capture in the wild, an ape appears before the members of an unspecified academy to describe his evolution into their cultivated guest speaker. Dubbed Red Peter, he recalls his capture on the Gold Coast, the sensation of the shots that felled him, his journey across the ocean to Europe inside a closely guarded cage, and his determined efforts to find his way out of his confinement by mimicking the crew that taught him by example how to spit, drink, and speak. Much as Heine ridicules through exaggeration the bigot's contempt for the Jew, Kafka literalizes the simian imagery in which the Jew was often cast. But all his emotional investment is in the ape. No one could say about him what was said about Heine: that he internalized the standards of the enemy.[24]

The ape's attitude is as generous to his captors as their treatment had been cruel to him. Wonderfully urbane, he registers the indignity of having been made to ape the Gentiles, while accepting full responsibility for deciding to make the switch and become human: "I could never have achieved what I have done had I been stubbornly set on clinging to my origins, to the remembrance of my youth. In fact, to give up being stubborn was the supreme commandment I laid upon myself, free ape as I was. I submitted myself to that yoke." Since he stands closer than does his audience to their common origins, he knows things they may be forgetting. "[Everyone] on earth feels a tickling at the heels; the small chimpanzee and the great Achilles alike."[25] The grotesque features of this parody—the ape addressing his vanquishers—are sweetened thanks to the far lower levels of sensitivity and thoughtfulness in the society of his betters.

It is easy to see the assimilating Jew under the ape's disguise—for instance, in the extended sequence where he tells how he first proved his adaptive capacities by drinking schnapps from a bottle. "The smell of it revolted me; I forced myself to it as best I could; but it took weeks for me to master my revulsion. This inward conflict, strangely enough, was taken more seriously by the crew than anything else about me."[26] Contempt for Gentile drunkenness was a trope of Jewish culture, which prided itself on relegating the consumption of alcohol to prescribed religious functions. Yet if the anomalies of Jewish assimilation inspired this parody, its Jewishness is nowhere made explicit. In this ape, one also can see Freud's human patients, ensnared by the demands of, in a word, civilization.

Kafka does not sentimentalize the primitive wild, and the ape understands that although adopting human form gives him greater agency than he could have had as a jungle creature, there is no ultimate liberation from constraint. He deliberately does not use the word freedom, nor does he any longer seek the actual greater freedom of movement. He has met human beings who yearn for it, but thinks that they are too frequently betrayed by the word:

> As freedom is counted among the most sublime feelings, so the corresponding disillusionment can be also sublime. In variety theaters I have often watched, before my turn came on, a couple of acrobats performing on trapezes high in the roof. They swung themselves, they rocked to and fro, they sprang into the air, they floated into each other's arms, one hung by the hair from the teeth of the other. "And that too is human freedom," I thought, "self-controlled movement." What mockery of holy Mother Nature! Were the apes to see such a spectacle, no theater walls could stand the shock of their laughter.[27]

Freud came to terms, mournfully but realistically, with the sacrifice of libido, eroticism, and swinging from the trees that was the cost of civilization. To our ape, in contrast, those lost freedoms were not so terrific to begin with, which makes people's attempt to win them back ridiculous at best. It is always unsettling to see residual animal aspects in human nature; to see human acrobatics from a simian point of view can make more than the apes laugh.

Yet ultimately the ape, like Kafka's other creature protagonists—Gregor Samsa the insect, the burrowing mole, the investigating dog, or Josephine of the mouse people—elicits more empathy in the reader than comedy can tolerate. Whereas the human heroes of Kafka's works are kept at arm's length in a way that mirrors their impersonal relations with others, his creatures are so intimately conceived that they pull us into their predicament and hearts. Comedy needs enough detachment from its subject to allow for the enjoyment of its playfulness. If Heine's comedy is overtaken by anger, Kafka's is overtaken by grief.

Thus, of the two possibilities open to him, the ape has chosen the variety stage over the zoo, and concludes his report with a description of how he ends his days.

> When I come home late at night from a banquet, or from some scientific society, or a friendly get-together, a little half-trained little chimpanzee is waiting up for me, and I take my pleasure with her after the apish fashion. I have no wish to see her by day; you see, she has the crazy, confused look of the trained animal in her eyes; I am the only one to recognize it, and I cannot endure it.
>
> In any case, I have on the whole achieved what I wanted to achieve. Do not say it was not worth the trouble. Besides, I am not asking for a judgment from any human, my only wish is to make these insights more widely known; I am simply reporting; to you, too, honoured gentlemen of the Academy, I have been simply making a report.[28]

The ape's refusal of pity is belied by the sympathy he feels for the creature that is just beginning the transformative process he has successfully traversed. By the point where the ape says, "I cannot bear it," the comic potential of the story has dissolved, and the bewildered half-broken animal stares out at us with an insane look in her eye.

■ The same pressures that produced *taufjuden*—baptized Jews who appeared to continue in their Jewish ways, somewhat like Marranos, the secret Jews who outlasted the Spanish and Portuguese Inquisition, but now were tolerated though seen as equally suspect by both Christians and Jews—fueled German Jewish humor. Taufjuden humor claimed the right to mock from the perspective of Jew or Gentile, or the perspective of both or neither—demonstratively free, yet aware of the forces that had brought it into being. Feeling threatened, Jews sublimated their anxieties in joking, which did not eliminate the threat. In Heine and Kafka, warnings against the limits of comedy emerge from the comedy itself. This is the quality that seemed prophetic in retrospect, when their premonitions were actualized by fellow Germans, and to an extent far beyond their imagining.

German Jewish humor influenced all other branches of Jewish culture. The man who stood at the helm of modern Yiddish culture in Poland, I. L. Peretz (1852–1915), came to regret what he considered the excessive influence of Heine while he tried to find his own literary voice. But no such qualms troubled other Yiddish writers who likewise discovered literature through Heine. The humor magazines published in New York City by Yiddish immigrants at the turn of the twentieth century regularly featured translations from Heine and imitations of Heine (some unacknowledged). In 1918, a group of these writers put out an eight-volume Yiddish edition of Heine's work—the only such literary tribute in U.S. Yiddish letters—reflecting not only the esteem in which the German writer was held but also a publisher's (no doubt exaggerated) estimation of his public appeal.

It is worth noting, however, that the introduction to these collected works casts Heine as a "tragic Jewish poet, perhaps the most tragic poet who every climbed the sacred mount of the muses. . . . Tragic in his poetry, his life, his loves, his suffering, his pathos, his thought, his ridicule, his cynicism, his sanctity, his pain, and his death."[29] In this reappraisal of Heine's comic writing, one can sense the catastrophic impact of the First World War on Jewish sensibilities, but perhaps also something of the difference between Yiddish and German Jewish humor.

By the lights of Yiddish humor—our next subject—Heine's humor *was* tragic.

Yiddish Heartland

A skeleton is shown into the doctor's office.
The doctor says: "*Now* you come to me?"

—Heard from Yosl Bergner, in Yiddish, Tel Aviv, 2012

The Yiddish humor of the East European Jew, or *Ostjude*, was as different from the German *Judenwitz* as *aleph* and *kometz-aleph* are from alpha and omega. In brief, Yiddish humorists peered out from inside Jewish life rather than, like Heine's narrator in "The Baths of Lucca," from outside in. This made their mockery not necessarily kinder but certainly more intricate and better informed. While the German language developed the stereotype of the "rootless cosmopolitan"—the Jew who is nervously trying to fit in while everywhere displaced—Yiddish conjured up a stuck-in-the-mud Jewish nation that was only belatedly lifting up its head.

One homely example of the distinction is the nose—the same nose that stigmatizes the Jew in the German writings of Heine, but that makes a very different sort of appearance in the 1905 story "Two Anti-Semites" by the Yiddish writer Sholem Aleichem.

In this story, the telltale protuberance appears on the face of a traveling salesman, Max Berliant (not quite "Brilliant").

Max has lately begun to sample the forbidden pleasures of the surrounding Gentile world. Travel through Russia, though a mere baby step on the road to assimilation as portrayed by Heine, nevertheless affords Max the chance to shed some of his Jewishness while evading the opprobrium of a watchful community. He is therefore annoyed by the intimate insinuations that his nose evokes from fellow Jews who squeeze into his share of a train compartment.

By the time of the story, though, Max has something even bigger to worry about: the 1903 killing spree in Kishinev—a vicious mass attack on Jews that had occurred in the same territory he is about to traverse:

> It must surely have happened to you while sitting on a train that you passed the place where some great catastrophe has occurred. You know in your heart that you are safe because lightning doesn't strike twice in the same spot. Yet you can't help remembering that not so long ago trains were derailed at this very point, and carloads of people spilled over the embankment. You can't help knowing that here people were thrown out head first, over there bones were crushed, blood flowed, brains were splattered. You can't help feeling glad that you're alive; it's only human to take secret pleasure in it.[1]

In this passage, Sholem Aleichem is deploying the Aesopian strategy that writers in Russia adopted to avoid czarist censorship, transposing a hypothetical railway accident for the brutal images of Kishinev: the first pogrom of the twentieth century and the first whose images of butchered bodies were disseminated by newspapers. The narrator invites us to experience Max's anxiety and relief—*there, but for the grace of God, lies* my *ravaged corpse*—while noting his hubris in trying to separate himself from the Jewish community—a serious taboo in traditional Judaism—during a time of national danger. Max is clever. As the train penetrates the region of peril, he gets off at a station and buys a copy of the *Bessarabian*, a regional anti-Semitic paper said to have incited local pogroms. Once back in the compartment, he stretches out on the bench, and drawing the newspaper over his face, reckons that he is safe from interference. "What a great way to get rid of Jews and at the same time keep a seat all to myself."

The reader can guess the rest. Another Jewish salesman enters the compartment, but unlike Max, this one, Patti Nyemchik by name, can't get enough of his fellow Jews and enjoys entertaining them with funny stories. Here he has stumbled on to one in the making! Taking in the scene—"during his sleep, the newspaper had slipped off Max's face to reveal his stigma"—Patti steps out on the platform to buy his own copy of the *Bessarabian*; once back in the compartment, he assumes Max's identical position on the opposite bench.

After a night of torturing dreams, Max wakes up, disoriented. He touches his nose and finds it gone—with a copy of the newspaper in its place. When he catches sight of the person on the opposite bench, he thinks it must be himself, but is at a loss to grasp the meaning of his out-of-body self. As he slowly comes to, his stirring wakes Patti, who smiles across at his fellow "anti-Semite" and tentatively starts whistling a popular Yiddish tune. Soon they are both singing it aloud,

Afn pripetchik brent a fayerl . . . , a little fire burns in the old woodstove, and the teacher sits reciting with the children the sounds of the Hebrew alphabet, *aleph* and *kometz-aleph*. The comedy of errors resolved, the two Jews continue on their journey, the more secure for being in harmony.

Is it any wonder that by the time of this story's publication, Sholem Aleichem—the Hebrew-Yiddish pen name means "peace be upon you," or in a word, "welcome!"—had become the Jews' most beloved writer, overcoming their increasing internal factionalism with his near-universal appeal? Like Patti, he enjoyed entertaining his fellow Jews with stories and jokes—a kind of company salesman whose product line was comedy. But this was a comedy that fed off the disquiet that it temporarily seemed to dispel.

Modernity, in the form of increased economic opportunity and social mobility, had simultaneously undermined Jewish social cohesion. Gentiles, meanwhile, were channeling some of *their* insecurities into violence against the "stranger in their midst." The comforting harmony of "Afn Pripetchik" was itself based on a flimsy premise, since the song was a fairly recent composition by the Kiev lawyer Mark Warshawski (1848–1907), and Sholem Aleichem, who had helped to popularize it, knew that no one could possibly mourn the antiquated Jewish education it sentimentalized. What is more, educated readers would have recognized in Max's dream the dark humor of Nikolay Vasilyevich Gogol's Russian story "The Nose," in which the feature in question is unaccountably shaven off a client's face to assume a life of its own. While the crisis in Sholem Aleichem remains safely on *this* side of grotesque, in actual life the Jewish presence in Russia was evoking hostility more disturbing than anything in Gogol's fiction.

On the basis of this story and others like it, more than one critic has described the effect of Sholem Aleichem's humor as "being awakened from nightmare," a kind of self-soothing that parents try to develop in their children to calm the terrors of life. In her study of child development, the psychoanalyst Selma Fraiberg introduces us to "Laughing Tiger," an imaginary companion invented by a two-year-old to calm her fear of animals. The creature never scares children and never bites, and you see its teeth only because it is laughing benignly. Fraiberg speculates that the transformation of a wild into an obedient beast "is probably a caricature of the civilizing process the little girl is undergoing," and that her make-believe gives her a kind of control over a danger that had left her helpless and anxious.[2] The U.S. comedian Mel Brooks offers a similar connection between fear and "civilization" in his comic routine of the two-thousand-year-old man. Asked about the principal means of transportation in his younger days, Brooks answers, "Fear. An animal would growl, you'd go two miles in a minute."[3] Along the same lines, Sholem Aleichem's humor, often called "laughter through tears," is more accurately understood as laughter through fears.

■ Born in 1859 in one Ukrainian Jewish town and raised in another, Sholem Rabinovich turned his given name into a term of common greeting as though he were standing on the doorstep welcoming one and all into his world. Thanks to the language in which he wrote, he remained bound to the Yiddish-speaking society. But there was also something of Max in him: the author was not identical with his fictional persona.

At the age of seventeen, Rabinovich was hired by a wealthy Jewish landowner to serve as a live-in secretary and tutor to the man's only daughter. Within a few years, pupil and instructor married, at first against the father's wishes. Happily, reconciliation ensued, and when his father-in-law died, the aspiring and now-wealthy writer was able to take up residence in Kiev, a city that was legally out of bounds to all but a privileged minority of Russian Jews. There he began a serious literary career while enjoying, albeit briefly, an affluent life. His longtime literary associate Yehoshua Ravnitski recalls that at their first meeting, he had trouble reconciling the homespun author he had been reading with the dandy in white spats who stood before him. Incongruities were the stuff of Rabinovich's life.

The man who became known as Sholem Aleichem liked to trace his comic genius to a childhood talent for mimicry; his earliest work, he said, was an alphabetized list of his stepmother's curses that won her over by making her laugh. His audience was meant to believe that in similar fashion, he had continued to pick up from commonplace Jews the sayings, anecdotes, and stories that he then artlessly repackaged for their enjoyment. And indeed, his male and female monologists, speaking "in their own voices," became beloved personalities in their own right. His fellow writer Yosef Haim Brenner called him a unique amalgam, a poet who was "a living essence of the folk itself."[4] He played the role so well that the extent of his influence on the folk's perception of itself went largely unnoticed.

In fact, Sholem Aleichem revolutionized Jewish culture more profoundly than any figure of his time. Almost single-handedly, he invented a Jewish people that laughed its way through crisis and an imaginary Jewish town, Kasrilevke, whose very name connoted merry pauperdom. His comic protagonists Menahem-Mendl, Sheyne-Sheyndl, and Tevye the Dairyman became national prototypes like the biblical Abraham, Esther, and Job. What Heine had celebrated as the "sabbath spirit" of the Jews was now presumed to function not as a sacred interval from the rest of the week but rather as an innate capacity for transmuting humiliation, subjugation, misery, and dread into funniness. This image would later be used in film and story to deactivate even the horrors of the Holocaust, though the salvific properties of laughter had clearly failed to save the population that allegedly sought refuge in it. Sholem Aleichem was not merely the alchemist but also the inventor of a putatively magical people.

Historians of the so-called Age of Nationalism that culminated in the First World War point to the heightened importance of a sustaining national culture in the struggle for the sovereignty of ethnic minorities like the Poles, Lithuanians, and Ukrainians. The national cohesion of Jews, who lived outside their ancestral territory, was even more dependent than those others on the nonpolitical underpinnings of peoplehood such as common language and literature. Sholem Aleichem's "fictional territory" of Jewish towns and cities with train compartments as their mobile prayer houses was a brilliant surrogate for national autonomy, and it was duly harnessed by all the emerging Jewish national movements of the time—including Zion-

Sholem Aleichem's spirit avowedly influenced the art of Marc Chagall, who later brought a modernist touch to the scenery and costumes he designed for the dramatic productions of Sholem Aleichem. Chagall's paintings of a fiddler, including this one of the violinist on a rooftop, became the iconic image for the Broadway musical that was based on Sholem Aleichem's stories of Tevye the Dairyman. Marc Chagall, *The Green Violinist*. © 2012 Artists Rights Society (ARS), New York / ADAGP, Paris and CNAC/ MNAM/Dist. RMN–Grand Palais / Art Resource, NY.

ism, which he actively promoted. The consummate insider and virtuoso of the insider's language, Sholem Aleichem seemed to offer a complete contrast to Heine—and so he did, until he was forced into exile from the Russia he had so ingeniously reimagined as his own. At that point, the homey language that had been his insulation betrayed the degree of his displacement. Once Jews abandoned Yiddish, they could no more understand the intricacies of his humor than could any Gentile.

■ To understand where Sholem Aleichem sprang from, I need to make a brief excursion into eastern European Jewish history as an incubator of modern Jewish humor.

Forays into the sources of Jewish comedy usually focus on institutions like the Purim *shpil*—a skit or performance marking the festival of Purim—and the *badkhen* or *marshalik*—the master of ceremonies called into service at celebrations and weddings. Both date from about the sixteenth century, when Jewish communities began selectively incorporating entertainments adapted from surrounding populations. Both provided opportunities for mostly amateur musical, poetic, and thespian performers. Some of the Purim scripts and badkhen songs became standard folk repertoire, and were later adapted by modern playwrights, poets, musicians, and writers who likewise worked in Yiddish, the everyday language. Studies and compendiums of this material show boundaries between folk and individual attribution remaining fluid well past the invention of the rotary printing press.

In western and central Europe, Jews had begun to speak and study in local languages by the end of the eighteenth century. The case was otherwise in the more populous Jewish communities of the Russian Empire, which remained mostly Yiddish speaking for about another century. There, Jews were concentrated mostly in towns, or shtetlach (singular, shtetl), where they formed substantial fractions, if not majorities, of the population. "Literacy" continued to refer to literacy in traditional Hebrew-Aramaic sources, studied mostly by boys in Jewish elementary schools and yeshivas.

This is not to say that Jewish society was immune to change. Whereas in France and Germany the impulse for change came mainly and directly from without, among eastern European Jews it could bubble up in autochthonous form in towns and cities where Jews constituted significant minorities. At the risk of compressing what scholars have gone to great lengths to distinguish and develop in detail, we can trace at least three powerful indigenous movements that vied for influence, each of them enriching Yiddish humor with mockery of the others.

Pressing in from the West, the Enlightenment, in the specifically Jewish form known as Haskalah, was a reformist movement requiring Jews to undertake the behavioral and ideational changes that could make them worthier of citizenship, were it ever to be on offer. In common with other modernizers, Maskilim, "Enlighteners," believed in progress, sometimes at the expense of inherited traditions and assumptions. Because they advanced their arguments in Jewish languages—Hebrew and Yiddish—they formed part of the cultural renaissance that transformed Jewish life from within. Almost all Maskilim favored Hebrew and used Yiddish only when stooping to conquer. Traffic between Hebrew and Yiddish characterized the Haskalah along with its humor throughout.

Warding off this Westernizing trend was a second movement, Hasidism (roughly, pietism). Originating in the eighteenth century, it had much in common with the Romantic movement in culture, typified by a rebellion against traditional authority—in this case, the authority of the rabbinate—and the elevation of intuition or emotion over reason. Revivalist and fundamentalist rather than progressive, Hasidism drew men together around charismatic leaders, the first of whom, and the acknowledged founder of the movement, was Israel ben Eliezer, known as the Baal Shem Tov (1698–1760). It also took inspiration from Jewish mysticism, popularizing the latter's elitist and esoteric emphases by encouraging unmediated, joyous apprehension of the divine.

The third group—Misnagdim, literally "opponents"—upheld traditional standards of Jewish self-discipline, observance, and study against Hasidic populists, on the one hand, and Maskilic enlighteners, on the other. The leading exponent of Misnagdic thought was Rabbi Elijah ben Solomon (1720–97), known as the Gaon of Vilna. His attempt to excommunicate Hasidim points up the intensity of friction among the warring factions; his failure to stop the spread of Hasidism indicates that the historical processes were beyond any Jewish authority's control.

Rivalry among these movements was fueled not only by vying ideas of what was best for the Jewish people but also by deep cultural divisions. When sociolinguists in the twentieth century began marking dividing lines, or isoglosses, on the dialectic map of the Yiddish language, they discovered an almost-exact correspondence between the boundaries that separated Hasidic from Misnagdic strongholds and much older ones separating southeastern from northeastern or "Lithuanian" dialects of Yiddish. Even today, among Jewish descendants from different regions of Russia, Poland, and Galicia, the skilled observer may recognize ancestral traces of their respective cultural dispositions. Nonetheless, while various strands of Jewish humor may still be distinguished at their source, there was obvious interpenetration among them: much of what time has joined together is here retroactively drawn apart.

■ Haskalah Humor

It was to be expected that Jewish Enlightenment satire would draw on the literary genres and tropes of its European counterpart. The hypocrites skewered in the plays of the French dramatist Molière turn up as the villains of Jewish bourgeois comedy, concealing their cupidity and malice under the guise of pious discourse and dress. The withering critique of the Catholic Church by French Enlightenment thinkers like Denis Diderot and Voltaire is redirected to the rabbinic oligarchy and its Hasidic challengers alike. Do Hasidic rebbes—as opposed to learned rabbis—presume to inspire rather than instruct? They may be cultivating ignorance in order to exploit the credulity of their followers. Do they comfort barren women with promises of fertility? It instead may be their physical interventions that guarantee the efficacy of their prophecies. In Yiddish Enlightenment comedy, German-speaking medical students outwit Hasidic charlatans in their bid for the daughters of the Jewish bourgeoisie, while earthy servants flirt and find their natural partners without the services of matchmakers. Sartorially, linguistically, politically, and domestically, this kind of comedy delights in upending established orders.

The title of Joseph Perl's *Revealer of Secrets* (1819) telegraphs its intention of demystifying the hocus-pocus of Hasidic wonder rabbis. Composed as an epistolary novel (in Hebrew, subsequently transposed by the author into Yiddish), the work details the scheme of several Hasidic enthusiasts to gain possession of a seditious anti-Hasidic book—which happens to be an exposé of Hasidism by a certain Joseph Perl. Since the fictional correspondents quote from genuine Hasidic texts, and since their letters allude to an actual conflict involving the author, the work invites readers to mistake at least part, if not all, of its satire for truth. The mockery ranges from crude devices for deflating exaggerated reputations, as when one Hasid writes to another that he was privileged to accompany their sainted leader to the outhouse, to sharper critiques of Hasidic obduracy, deviousness, immorality, and criminality.

Perl (1773–1839) was among the most intriguing and disturbing figures of the Jewish Enlightenment, exemplifying the creative potential as well as moral hazards of that transitional moment. Had he not, as a teenager, been attracted by the fervor of Hasidism, he might not later have tried so aggressively to expose its seductive appeal. Committed to educating Jews as useful citizens, he received government help to establish a school that introduced science, the study of language, and a modern approach to traditional sources. Yet he was prevented from publishing some of his writings during his lifetime, just as he tried to prevent Hasidim from publishing theirs. He was denounced to czarist authorities, and in turn he denounced others—including the Hasidic rabbi Israel of Ruzhin for alleged complicity in killing a Jewish informer. His Yiddish translation of Henry Fielding's *Tom Jones*, unpublished during his lifetime, provides the model for some of the dodges and subterfuges of his own fiction.

Perl was flirting with one kind of danger by provoking reprisals from Hasidim, but with another kind by exposing his fellow Jews to hostile Polish scrutiny:

> One nobleman asked if he knew the reason why the Jews sway during the Tfile, and the agent said, "I don't know." The nobleman said to him, "I'll tell you the reason—because the Tfile is like intercourse. That's what's written in the book *Likutey Yekorim*.[5]

The fictional nobleman, alluding to a common devotional practice during the central Amidah prayer in Jewish religious services, quotes accurately from a treasury of sayings by Yekhi'el Mikhl of Zlotshev (1726–81), whose mystical fervor is conveyed in the image of cleaving to the Lord. Such erotic tropes, though unexceptional in Hasidic literature, might appear depraved to those controlling their political fate. Perl's satire exploits his intimate knowledge of Jewish life and lore without apparent thought for corresponding failings on the part of those in power—or their failure to distinguish between the progressive Jew, represented by Perl, and his allegedly reactionary coreligionists.

Indeed, Maskilim varied greatly in how much they trusted local authorities over fellow Jews; by the latter part of the nineteenth century, especially after the pogroms of 1881–82, few were as prepared as Perl to side with the Gentile perspective. Gentler in this respect was the Maskilic comedy of Abraham Goldfaden (1840–1908), affectionately known as the father of the modern Yiddish theater, whose career had its improbable start when he was a student at the Zhitomir rabbinical seminary and starred as the female lead in a school production of a newly circulating Yiddish drama. This was before the advent of a Jewish theater, and the play was never produced during its author's lifetime.[6] The government-run seminary was meant to educate modern Russian-speaking rabbis and teachers, but on graduating Goldfaden saw greater opportunity for cultural advancement in Western-style literature and dramatic entertainment.

Theater historians date the birth of the professional Yiddish stage from the evening in 1876 when Goldfaden performed comic sketches in a beer garden in Jassy, Romania. By the following year he was touring with his own Yiddish troupe, performing a repertoire of his own plays. Goldfaden was unlikely to overestimate the benevolence of the czarist government, which imposed an official ban on Yiddish productions in 1883 that forced him to light out for London and later New York.

One of Goldfaden's best creations was Kuni-Leml, in the comedy *The Two Kuni-Lemls* (*leml* being a little lamb)—the male equivalent of the old maid in the marriage-broker joke I cited earlier, "She's ugly and old, she squints, and has bad teeth . . . You needn't lower your voice . . . [since] she's deaf as well." In a culture that hadn't yet learned to call cripples "disabled," and a theater that represented moral imperfections as physical defects, no caricature could have been crueler than Goldfaden's description of Kuni-Leml, a twenty-year-old Hasid blind in one eye, lame in one foot, and a stutterer.

And Kuni-Leml was simple to the point of idiocy. When handsome Max, a university student, disguises himself as Kuni-Leml in a plot to secure parental approval for his, Max's, marriage to their daughter Khayele (aka Carolina), he deceives not only the parents but also the infatuated and clueless Hasid, who lets himself be persuaded that Max is the "real" Kuni-Leml. Their encounter is a manic version of the ageless routine that Sholem Aleichem evokes in "Two Anti-Semites," where disguise tests the very notion of identity.

> KUNI-LEML: I m-meant to ask . . . for example, if I walk down the street and someone calls out to me, "Reb K-kuni-Leml! Reb K-kuni-Leml!" should I answer or not?
>
> MAX (*in an angry tone*): No, you m-mustn't answer, since you're not K-kuni-Leml! Now r-run along home![7]

By thus exposing his rival, Max convinces Carolina's father to recognize the religious folly represented by the young Hasid. In the final scene, a chorus of university students chases the Hasidim off the stage, completing the triumph of modernity over obscurantism.

Even though Goldfaden's original title, *The Fanatic*, almost certainly took aim at the obscurantists, the operetta he based on his play moderated the severity of the critique. When the curtain falls in the musical version, Kuni-Leml, having secured a bride of his own, is singing along with the chorus, and the hubris of Max the modernizer is shown up as almost equal to the stubbornness of the religious believer.[8] A 1977 Israeli film adaptation, *Kuni Leml in Tel Aviv*, is similarly ambivalent toward easy assumptions of progress, and for similar reasons, suggesting that the threats to Jewish life from the temptations of modernity almost outweigh the perceived corruptions of entrenched tradition. Ultimately in both versions, music and dance sweep up the antagonists in familial as well as cultural comic harmony.

■ Hasidic Humor

Less obvious than the role of the Haskalah in the development of modern Jewish comedy is the role of the Haskalah's favorite target, Hasidism. We may not customarily associate Hasidic ecstasy with laughter, but we should consider how, like ecstasy, laughter too overcomes indignities through an altered state of mind. The believer subordinates the material considerations of earthly life to the quest for divine perfection; the ironist makes fun of the gap between the two. To elevate the spiritual over the material, transcendence over immanence, Hasidic teachers employ paradox, contradiction, and incongruity—the very features that Freud identifies as staples of joking. Both mystic and comedian aspire to get the better of a world they are powerless to reform.

The *Tales* of the Hasidic master storyteller Nahman, mentioned briefly in the previous chapter, are compendiums of inversion whose narrator tries to wean us from trust in manifest reality to allegedly profounder levels of perception. In Nahman's most famous story, seven beggars bless a newly married couple with the words, "May you be as I am." That is, the blind beggar confers the gift of insight, the hunchback the ability to shoulder the world, the stutterer—following Moses in the Bible—the key to cosmic mysteries, and so forth. Beggars become benefactors, presenting ostensible deformities as moral advantages while implicitly showing the pursuit of sensual pleasure as *corrupting* the senses. As in comedy, Nahman upends our expectations through dramatic reversals. In another tale, featuring a contest between a simple man and a wise one, we see how the latter cannot achieve through his merits what the former attains by trust. The wise man, an ideal Maskil, is exposed as a restless, compulsively miserable perfectionist, misled by his skepticism into self-destruction; the simpleton takes on honor and authority by joyously obeying the summons of "the King."

One scholar has compared this dialectic tactic to the Talmudic expression *adraba—ipkha mistabra*, yet the opposite (of what was just stated) is the more reasonable. "It is the signal that the student must awaken to a logical reversal, . . . reconsider everything, distinguish anew between truth and falsehood."[9]

The aphorism attributed to Nahman, "Nothing is as whole as a broken heart," invites us to experience language itself as paradox; indeed, Hasidic storytelling occasionally severs altogether the relation of language to meaning. Deficiencies of conventional prayer are conveyed in the story (that has analogues in other cultures) of a boy whose whistle pierces the gates of heaven during the closing service of Yom Kippur, after the entreaties of the rabbi have failed to do so. In a more extreme version of this anecdote, a pious but ignorant water carrier prays passionately by intoning a single word, *tamei*—meaning "impure," "unclean." To protect the man from public mockery, and in deference to religious propriety, the rabbi of Kotsk asks him to substitute the contrasting word, *tahor*, meaning "pure," as in pure of heart. The water carrier tries to follow this advice but fails; when he reports back to the saintly Kotsker that his prayer has been ruined in the attempt, the latter gives him permission to return to tamei. Sincerity trumps significance.[10]

Such habits of inversion in Hasidic storytelling were transmitted from redemptive fools to their successors, zany comedians. Through this same kind of verbal inversion the Marx Brothers would later overturn polite society, refreshing its language and puncturing the pretensions of people who think *they* are in command.

Another spring of corrective humor welled up from within Hasidism itself—this one aimed at the movement's own excesses. A rich fund of stories arose around Hershele Ostropolier, hailing from the town of Ostropol in the Hasidic heartland. Hershele, a semilegendary prankster in the universal tradition of the trickster, is alternately on the right and wrong side of morality. He is capable of devouring a dish of dumplings that a mother begs him to leave for her hungry children, or instructing a browbeaten husband to reform his wife—with a whip. In this respect he owes much to Germany's famed jester Till Eulenspiegel, who tricks the stingy out of their money, insults the high and mighty, and pays back other mischief-makers in kind. But cultural differences play their part. Where the German trickster is an archetypal social outcast, Hershele supports his wife and children. Intent on exposing the underside of his society, Eulenspiegel often has other people (including Jews) eat his excrement.[11] Hershele, much more reserved, substitutes scatological rhetoric for the thing itself:

> A wealthy Jew refuses Hershele's appeal for a handout. Instead of a curse, Hershele rewards him with a blessing: "You and your children and your children's children will remain prosperous until the end of days." The tightwad wants this sanction explained, so Hershele obliges him: "When a pauper goes to the outhouse and accidentally drops a kopek into the pit, he would probably not reach in to pick it up. If a wealthier man attending to his needs dropped even a ruble into the excrement, he would almost certainly not stoop to recover it. Since it is said of the Lord of Hosts, "The silver is mine and the gold is mine," having once dropped, say, fifty thousand rubles into you, would He be likely to dirty Himself by stooping to retrieve it?"[12]

Hershele pulls the comic lever here by means of a quotation from the prophet Haggai (2:18) to the effect that prosperity—all the silver and gold—is God's to bestow, which would be familiar to the average synagogue goer. The semantic drop from high to low, from Haggai into the pit, corresponds to the deflation of the miser—although whether the vulgar Hershele is offending religion or acting as its worldly standard-bearer is left ambiguous. In this connection, it is worth noting that according to Chaim Bloch (1881–1973), a scholar of Jewish folklore who assembled a well-researched collection of Hershele stories, those who had known the man attested that of his two miens—the pious and roguish—the former was dominant.[13]

Trickster humor was by no means confined to Hasidic territory. Among other wits who became known by name, one might mention Shmerl Snitkever and Leybenyu Gotsvunder in Hershele's Podolia (Ukraine), Motke Chabad of Lithuania, and Shayke Fefer of Poland. Jewish beggars, or schnorrers, endorsed by a religion that requires high levels of giving, generated a brand of comic insolence by demanding gratitude from their benefactors. In the previous chapter, we saw how Heine's Moses Lump invites a compliant Rothschild to polish his sabbath lamp. In Yiddish joking, a beggar turned away because the master of the house has suffered a financial reversal retorts, "So because he's had a bad week, why should *my* family go hungry?" Asked to return the following day because of a lack of money at hand, the schnorrer objects, "If only you knew what a fortune I've lost by extending credit."

When the twentieth-century Yiddish writer Isaac Bashevis Singer (1902–91) began speaking before U.S. audiences, he developed a routine that contrasted the scarcity of English terms for poor person (pauper or beggar) with the abundance of its Yiddish equivalents: accompanying the plain *oreman* and *evyon* are the burned-out *nisrof*, the *farshpiler* who has gambled away his money, the once-wealthy *yored* who has lost his fortune, the *betler* and *schnorrer* who have turned poverty into a profession, the "mistress over a head of cabbage," the "doyenne of shovel and poker," or "one for whom the whole year is Passover—he hasn't enough for a slice of bread." In this comedy of inversion, U.S. prosperity is put to shame by the inventive richness of Jewish poverty.

■ Misnagdic Humor

In addition to Enlightenment satire and Hasidism's multi-pronged comedy of inversion, a long tradition of rabbinic wit continued strong in the yeshiva circles of eastern Europe. Just as Samuel Johnson's educated male society of London became known for its table talk, rabbinic scholars were touted for their *sikhes khulin*—their demonstrations of rabbinic wit. The appetite for this sort of humor in Lithuanian Jewish circles matched the Hasidic taste for the magical exploits of their leaders. Indeed, early collections of Yiddish humor contain as many stories about clever rabbis as they do about tricksters and matchmakers.

The microscopic examination of texts that is the hallmark of Talmudic learning produced, in addition to centuries of creative exegesis, an appetite for verbal ingenuity and appreciation for subtleties of the language. Since Hebrew was not vocalized, rabbis could frequently pun on a word to make a point. In one famous (and nonhumorous) example from the

Talmudic Tractate Berakhot 64a, Rabbi Elazar says in the name of Rabbi Hanina, "'Students of the sages increase peace in the world,' as it is written, *vekhol banayikh limudey adonay, verav shlom banayikh*, And all your children shall be disciples of the Lord, And great shall be the happiness of your children (Isaiah 54:13). Do not read, 'your children' (*banayikh*) but rather 'those who build you up' (*bonayikh*)."[14] This idea—that scholars spread peace—was later often cited ironically. But the formula, "do not read X but rather Y," opened the door to myriad creative misreadings.

Another subgenre comprises anecdotes of how scholars refuse unwelcome petitioners and squelch impertinent critics:

> "But you approved my earlier commentary on the Book of Job," complains an author who has just been refused a rabbi's endorsement of his new book. "Well, you see, Job is different," replies the rabbi, "I thought that having already withstood so many hardships, he could survive another."

> A skeptic challenges the Malbim [acronym of the rabbi and scholar Meir Leibush ben Jehiel Mikhel Weiser, 1809–79] to tell him whether among all their ingenious legal fictions, the rabbis could not find a way of allowing smoking on the Sabbath. The Malbim replies, "Of course. If the burning end of the cigarette is placed in your mouth."

> A lawyer taunts the rabbi with a mock predicament: if the wall between heaven and hell collapses, which side

> should bear the cost of reconstruction? The rabbi replies: justice favors those in heaven, given that the fires of hell destroyed the wall. But the smooth-talking lawyers in hell would probably win the case.[15]

It goes without saying that the conservative purposes served by this wit were turned by opponents of the rabbis against what they took to be the absurd logic chopping of its practitioners.

In his study of jokes, the philosopher Ted Cohen highlights a special category of *hermetic* humor, which is accessible only to those versed in an arcane subject.[16] Much rabbinic, or "yeshivish," joking likewise rewards only insiders and shuts out Jews (let alone non-Jews) who are insufficiently steeped in Talmudic culture. The following joke's punch line is visual:

> At the height of a pogrom [a standard opening for modern Jewish joking], drunken thugs break into a house of study and make a rush at the boys who are at their prayers. When one of the thugs raises his axe over a yeshiva student, the intended victim utters the prayer for *kiddush hashem*—sanctification of the Holy Name—said by someone about to be killed for his faith. Momentarily spooked, his attacker demands that the other yeshiva boys tell him what his victim is saying. With lips compressed, they mutely motion the killer to continue what he is doing.[17]

Even supposing that listeners appreciated this subspecies of gallows humor, the person who laughs at the unspoken punch line would need to know, first, that Jewish law prohibits a blessing uttered in vain (*brokheh l'vatoleh*), and second, that one may not speak between the utterance of a prayer and its fulfillment. That obedience to these requirements would here result in the boy's murder is the morally absurd twist that scares up the laughter.

The familiar theme of this joke is the Jews' predilection for compounding the trouble they are in, but since part of the pleasure of jokes is intellectual, its hermetic nature heightens the pleasure of those who get it. In another version of the same story, a circumciser who is past his prime pronounces the blessing for circumcision and then mistakenly cuts the hand of the person holding the infant boy. When the man yelps in pain, the circumciser moans, "Oh, woe! A brokheh l'vatoleh!"

Those familiar with Yiddish joking—or for that matter, with any kind of male joking—may marvel that I have scanted eroticism and sex. Were these Jews so chaste, so observant of the commandments of modesty, that they avoided what dominates humor elsewhere? Yes and no. One evening in the 1970s when I dropped in to visit Professor Khone Shmeruk in Jerusalem—such visits were among the favorite evenings of my life—he and several guests who had assembled earlier, all male, were gathered around a thin book that they rapidly put away when I entered the room. Their schoolboy gesture piqued my curiosity. At my insistence, Khone later showed me Ignatz Bernstein's collection of Yiddish sayings, only not the huge classic volume with which I was familiar. It seems that in an effort to satisfy both his scholarly obligation and sense of propriety, Bernstein issued a separately published edition of erotic and scatological material.

Wouldn't you know that among all of Bernstein's efforts, this offprint *alone* has been rendered into English—though not

This New Year's greeting card shows a Jew reciting the blessing of *kaparoth* before Yom Kippur: "We ask of God that if we were destined to be the recipients of harsh decrees in the new year, may they be transferred to this chicken in the merit of this mitzvah of charity." The atonement fowl would then be ritually slain, and its equivalent value given as charity. Nicholas II's face superimposed on this impending sacrifice would have amused Russian Jews in New York, where the card was printed, and recipients in Russia, if censorship did not intervene. Rosh Hashanah Postcard. © C. Stern. Russia, Early 20th Century. Collection of Yeshiva University Museum.

everything turns out as funny in translation. *Vayber haltn, vos es shteyt* is rendered in English as "Women grasp what stands," but the Yiddish expression "as it stands" ordinarily applies to the text of the Bible. *Fraytik, iz der tokhes tsaytik*, "Friday, and the behind is ready," conflates the alleged custom of spanking Jewish elementary students on Fridays (so that they will behave over the sabbath) and prescribed pleasures of intercourse for the sabbath.[18] Anyway, you get the idea. Yiddish humor ventures into common male territory, but perhaps with more than the usual compunction. This is reason enough for me to honor the Yiddish scholars' tact.

■ Women's or Folk Humor

The masculine realms of Yiddish humor that I have been describing were complemented by a fourth, largely female domain where Sholem Aleichem claims to have gotten his start. As I mentioned earlier, in his autobiography he presents an alphabetical list of his stepmother's curses as his first literary work. The inventory keeps getting funnier, as common slurs like donkey, fool, and idiot cascade into lists like this one for the letter *pey*: *paskudniak* (nasty man), *partatsh* (bungler), *parkh* (scab head), *pustepasnik* (wastrel), *pupik* (belly button), *pipernoter* (viper), *pletsl* (small pastry), *petelele* (buttonhole), *pempik* (fatso), *pere-odm* (savage), and *pritchepe* (quarreler or sponger). Torrential diatribe may not be experienced as funny by its target but certainly makes for great comedy at secondhand.

Though Yiddish cursing was by no means the exclusive preserve of women, the culture ascribes to them a special talent for verbal abuse. This can range from simple expletives, like *a shvarts yor af dir* ("may you have a black year"—a year of misfortune), to such ingenious maledictions as, "May you lose all your teeth, except the one that torments you," or (to a man), "May you grow so rich that your widow's second husband never has to work for a living," whose pretzel twists show off their comic invention over and above the insult they deliver. With less formal education than men, women may have developed more freewheeling oral aggression. Men were wont to say that a hen that crows, a Gentile who speaks Yiddish, and a woman who studies Torah are not good merchandise.[19] Perhaps, then, as a way of getting even, the woman with "nine measures of speech" became a staple of Yiddish folklore, and the harridan housewife an archetype of Yiddish theater. The latter tradition was still going strong in the Yiddish-accented, tough-talking Bessie Berger of Clifford Odets's perennial U.S. favorite, *Awake and Sing!* (1935).

Women were also masters of proverbs, compressions of folk wisdom often adapted from classical Jewish texts or neighboring cultures. So highly did my mother value what she called *her* maxims that she left a handwritten list of them for each of her children under the heading "My Philosophy of Life." Her register included both Talmudic homilies like *a rahmen af gazlonim iz a gazlen af rahmonim* (kindness to the cruel is cruelty to the kind), and takeoffs on Talmudic sayings. Thus, "The world rests on three things—learning, prayer, and acts of loving kindness," becomes, in her ironic rendition, "The world rests on three things—money, money, and money." Where others might say, "Don't worry. It'll turn out all right," my mother would say, "Either the landowner will die or the dog will croak." This last punch line was the rabbi's reply to the question of why he had gambled his life on his ability to teach the landowner's dog to speak within the year. A recipient of this folk wisdom was expected to know the joke and hence to appreciate the ambiguity of my mother's reassurance.[20]

Sholem Aleichem plundered this long-standing treasure trove of invective and folk wisdom in fashioning his female monologists, like the distaff side in the husband-and-wife exchange of letters that constitutes his epistolary novel *The Letters of Menahem-Mendl and Sheyne-Sheyndl*. Menahem-Mendl, setting out from his native Kasrilevke (as we have seen, Sholem Aleichem's fictional paradigm of the Jewish shtetl) to make his family's fortune in the big city Yehupetz (modeled on Kiev, from which most Jews were barred), ricochets from one entrepreneurial or investment scheme to another, failing every time and rebounding after every failure. Critics have been undecided as to whether he personifies the indomitable Jewish messianic spirit or a parody of capitalism run amok, but there is less disagreement over the conservative nature of his long-suffering wife, burdened with children and the need to feed them. Where his letters abound with the new terminologies of the stock market, real estate, and brokerage, Sheyne-Sheyndl, buttressed by her ever-present mother, conveys a single message: cut your losses and return home. Her weapons of choice are her mother's proverbs. "My mother says dumplings in a dream are a dream and not dumplings." "The best dairy dish is a piece of meat." And more:

> No one ever made money by counting on his fingers. You know what my mother says, invest a fever and you'll earn consumption. Mark my words, Mendl, all your overnight Yehupetz tycoons will soon by the grace of God be the same beggars they were before. . . . I tell you, if a mad dog ate my heart, the creature would go crazy.[21]

We encountered this mad dog earlier in Agnon, and will do so again with humans or animals going mad.

■ What Yiddish Signified

Yiddish humor was no less affected than its German Jewish counterpart by the Jews' encounters with modernity, but Yiddish speakers experienced its paradoxes in *their* language, which retained its Jewishness as they shed some of theirs. The linguist Max Weinreich called Yiddish "the language of the way of the Shas," with Shas being an acronym for the six tractates of the Mishnah that form the core of the Talmud and thus the basis of rabbinic Judaism. Why else but to perpetuate a distinctive Jewish way of life would Jews have created a separate language, and how could that language fail to preserve some imprint of the idea of divine election and Torah imperatives, the hope of return to Israel, categories of kosher and treyf, sabbath and weekday, and so forth? Yiddish signified, in however attenuated a form, Judaism's many habits of mind and conduct.

While anti-Jewish humor mocked telltale accents of Yiddish as the mark of the Jew, Jewish humor mocked the attempts of Yiddish speakers to disguise it:

> A wealthy American Jewish widow, determined to rise in society, hires coaches in elocution, manners, and dress to help her shed her Yiddish accent and coarse Jewish ways. Once she feels ready, she registers at a restricted resort, enters the dining room perfectly coiffed, wearing a basic black dress with a single string of pearls, and orders a dry martini—which the waiter maladroitly spills on her lap. The woman cries: "Oy vey!—whatever *that* means!"

There are many iterations of this joke in which, as Freud puts it, "primitive nature breaks through all the layers of education," but this one adds the absurdity of trying to conceal what has just been revealed.[22]

Given the dependence of Yiddish on Jewishness, it is not surprising that Sholem Aleichem, the master of Yiddish humor, should have aimed his deadliest barbs at such defectors from the tribe. Almost everyone in his repertoire is accorded a measure of sympathy—the pimp from Buenos Aires, the hustling cardsharp, and an "emissary from the Land of Israel" who graces a Passover seder before making off with the maid and family silver. But no sympathy at all is extended to the Jew who refuses to join a prayer quorum. In one of these stories, Jewish passengers in a railway car are seeking a tenth man to complete a minyan so that a father can recite kaddish on the anniversary of the death of his son. The son had been hanged as a revolutionary after a trial that the father swears was rigged, and his mother had died of grief. A bereaved version of Patti, the father has eyes of the kind that "once you've seen you'll never ever forget: half-laughing and half-crying they were, or half-crying and half-laughing . . . if only he would unburden himself and let the tears out! But no, he insisted on being the very soul of gaiety." Like the song that reestablishes Jewish harmony in the story of "Two Anti-Semites," gathering a minyan for the recitation of the mourner's prayer will confirm that a besieged community is still holding its own in hostile terrain:

> In fact, there was a tenth person there. We just couldn't make up our minds if he was a Jew or a Christian. An uncommunicative individual with a gold pince-nez, a freckled face, and no beard. A Jewish nose but an oddly twirled, un-Jewish mustache. . . . From the start he had kept his distance from us. Most of the time he just looked out the window and whistled. Naturally, he was hatless, and a Russian newspaper lay across his knees.

The story's problem is simple: Can this young man be persuaded to join the minyan, helping to compensate—however partially—for the Jewish son who has been eliminated? Apparently not. He says: "Count me out!"[23]

Through the grieving father, Sholem Aleichem mounts his revenge as a dish served cold. Rather than pleading or ranting, the father tells the young man that he deserves a gold medal and, like Hershele in the joke about the outhouse, promises an explanation if he will join the minyan. The mourner himself then leads an afternoon service "that could have moved a stone," and afterward spins a chain of apparently disconnected stories—the first about a coachman who, because he turns out to be a Jew, makes possible a circumcision ceremony in a remote village, the second about a Gentile who prevents a fire on the sabbath because he happens *not* to be a Jew, and the third about a rabbi's son exempted from the military draft because he has open sores on his head. "And now tell me, my dear young friend," the mourner concludes, "do you understand your true worth? You were born a Jew, you'll soon be a goy, and you're already a running sore." The story's tagline is almost redundant: "At the very next station our tenth man slipped away."[24]

When all is said and done, the "very soul of gaiety" cannot maintain his sanguinity. The bereaved father speaks for the author, who knows that the young man who counts himself out of a prayer quorum is also destroying the community of Jewish joking. Unlike Heine, Börne, Kraus, and other German wits, Yiddish wits are not usually converts themselves but instead are forever anxious that their children might be. Hence, in collections of Yiddish wit, the many entries under the category of apostates, *meshumodim*:

> Four converts trade stories about why they converted. The first explains that he was the victim of a false accusation and converted to escape the harsh sentence he would otherwise have had to serve. The second confesses that his parents drove him wild with complaints about his lax Jewish observance, so he converted to spite them. The third gives a rambling account of falling in love with a Christian girl, a model of loveliness: he converted in order

> to marry her. The fourth pipes up: "Unlike the rest of you, I converted out of firm conviction that Christianity is a religion of a higher order . . ."
>
> "Oh, PLEASE!" the others interrupt him—"Save that for your goyishe friends!"[25]

Transvaluation of values is the minority's means of reasserting its agency; in Yiddish joking, the only inauthentic motive for conversion is the one that claims to be authentic. "Of course, I converted out of conviction," said the famed real-life scholar Daniel Abramovitch Chwolson, "the conviction that it is better to be Professor of Oriental Languages at the University of St. Petersburg than a *heder* teacher in Berdichev."[26] Jewish humor is never more anti-Gentile than when it confirms the reality of Jews turning Christian and never more nationalistic than when it admits Jewish infirmity.

■ Tempting as it is to represent Yiddish humor exclusively through Sholem Aleichem, his dominance did not prevent the rise of a generation of new comic writers. I will briefly introduce four.

Itsik Manger (1901–69) was born in Galicia into a family of tailors, made his reputation in Warsaw between the world wars, escaped the continent to spend World War II in England, and settled in Israel in 1958.

Moshe Nadir (1885–1943; né Isaac Reiss) arrived in New York from his native Galicia at age thirteen and could easily have made his reputation in English. For many years a mainstay of the Yiddish Communist daily *Freiheit*, he "repented" of his affiliation after the Hitler-Stalin pact of 1939. Nadir's widow, Genia, married Manger in 1951 and bequeathed both of their archives to the National Library in Jerusalem.

Moshe Kulbak (1896–1937) remained closest to his birthplace in Smorgon (Smarhon), a small town in today's Belarus about halfway between Vilna and Minsk. The political fate that divided those two cities between Poland and the Soviet Union in the period between the world wars also sealed Kulbak's destiny. Employed in the mid-1920s as a teacher in the Vilna Jewish Teacher's Seminary, Kulbak crossed the Polish border into the Soviet Union in 1928 to rejoin the larger part of his family and was executed there nine years later.

Among Yiddish writers, Isaac Bashevis Singer enjoyed the greatest international success, culminating in the 1978 Nobel Prize for Literature. Son of a small-town Polish rabbi and rabbi's daughter, and raised in Warsaw where he began working as a writer and translator, he arrived in the United States in 1935, but did not begin situating his stories in that country until the 1950s. The youngest of the four, he was raised the most traditionally, and drew from the richest fund of traditional lore, even as he was the most profane in its use.

Manger and Nadir made no secret of their indebtedness to Heine, the major influence from the sphere of German on all Yiddish writers, though each drew his own image of the "accursed poet"—Nadir in the United States affecting the high-mannered pose of a dandy, and Manger in the heartland of Yiddish assuming the persona of a troubadour-inebriate who expects to be forgiven his indelicacies as the by-product of his genius. For the first *Lexicon of Yiddish Literature*, Manger falsely cited Berlin as his birthplace and Rainer Maria Rilke as his main influence, but his signature as "Itsik" rather than the formal Isidore (as in his birth record) belied this association with German culture. Attracted alike by Heine's melodic harmonies and comic subversion, Manger developed his own poetic mixture of the sweet and tart in lyrics and ballads that domesticated transgressive subjects like the sainted Jesus, elevated the humble, and punctured the pompous.

Manger's most productive years were spent in Warsaw, where three hundred thousand Jews comprising about a third of the city constituted the most vibrant audience any Yiddish writer or playwright would ever have. This island of Jewishness in a once-friendlier but increasingly xenophobic Poland inspired a series of mock-biblical poems—*Chumash lider*—that transpose stories of Genesis and the Book of Ruth into the language and experience of eastern European Jews. Anachronism was Manger's beloved comic device for filling in gaps in the action, elevating minor characters and trimming patriarchs down to size. When Sarah complains to her husband, Abraham, about the indignity of having Hagar's child in the house while she, the mistress, is not getting any younger, Manger tweaks the biblical account:

> The Patriarch Abraham puffs at his pipe.
> And waits, then he says with a smile,
> "A broomstick, my dear, can be made to shoot
> If the Lord thinks it's worthwhile."[27]

Midrash had long since humanized and tried to interpret the enigmatic biblical text, but Manger's comic midrash in everyday Yiddish idiom shifts the focus from the miraculous pregnancy of the aging wife to the husband who boasts of his no less astounding virility.

The Jewish festival of Purim, mandated by the Megillah, the Scroll or Book of Esther, is traditionally celebrated by spoofs and masquerade; in keeping with custom, Manger's 1936 verse rendition, *Songs of the Megillah*, purports to be mischief-making on the model of Purim players in every age. As part of the fun, he pretends to restore to the narrative the neglected figure of Fastrigossa, a journeyman tailor who romances Esther before she is taken up by King Ahasuerus. Although the biblical story of the villainous Haman who plots to exterminate the Jews already conveys the fragile political status of Jews in exile, Manger finds its happy resolution still too triumphal for the Jews of Poland in the mid-1930s, when the play was written and performed. So Fastrigossa fails in his attempt to assassinate the king and is punished by hanging. Haman has his son trumpet news of the failed assassination in the nationalist paper he edits in an attempt to stir up pogroms.

Yoking Persia to Prussia makes the story funnier and frighteningly actual. The only time I saw this musical performed onstage, the loudest laugh greeted Fastrigossa's serenade to the girl that will never be his:

Remember, remember that rainy night
At the gate when we clung together,
And I whispered a secret in your ear
And we did not mind the weather?

> I whispered, "Esther, marry me,
> Let's elope to Vienna."[28]

Perhaps that allurement of Vienna reminded some audience members of similar fantasies they had nourished in their youth. The play concludes with a dirge sung by Fastrigossa's mother, accusing her son's former fiancée of having whored her way into royalty. Anachronism is at one and the same time Manger's means of bringing the story up to date—with references to contemporary anti-Semitism and class conflict—and rehearsing the comedy of a people overdetermined for tragedy.

Like Manger, Nadir cast himself as another maverick or "bad boy" of Yiddish, advertising his philosophical caprice. *Na dir* is Yiddish for "there you are," a pen name that may signify either gift or fillip, and in Nadir's case more likely the latter. Along with his even more talented colleague, the poet Moishe Leyb Halpern, Nadir made his name translating and imitating Heine for the Yiddish humor magazines of the Lower East Side, and then developed his own gallery of immigrant misfits in humorous sketches that he published in the Yiddish daily press. His parodies of "getting rich in America" generated a new Americanese. In the much performed and anthologized humoresque "My First Deposit," a worker tells of how he consigns twenty dollars to a bank, and then grows obsessive about its security to the point that he finally withdraws his money… and loses it to a pickpocket on the way home. Included in the dialogue between customer and bank teller are the words *detsol*, *itsenuf*, and *tsimposibl*, which thereby morph from mispronunciations of English into "literary" Yiddish. The public loved Nadir for his humor, and fellow poets adored his contributions to the language.

While some Yiddish writers of the interwar generation experienced the dislocations caused by U.S. freedoms, their counterparts in Russia were trying to skirt the narrowing confines of Soviet censorship. Kulbak had come on the scene as a rural troubadour, rejecting the stereotypical Talmudic bench squeezer, peripatetic middleman, or tubercular artisan for a "healthier" kind of Jew. The heroes of his early poems take to the road like vagabonds, toil the livelong day like ordinary peasants, and seek out earthy pleasures among the haystacks. His humor ripened when he came under Soviet rule, and turning more to prose than poetry, introduced the ironies that such Jewish adjustments might actually require. The culminating work of his abbreviated life was the comic novel *Zelmenyaners*, describing a Jewish family's Sovietization during the same years that coincided with Kulbak's own resettlement in Minsk. I will return to this novel in chapter 4.

Singer (who wrote under the name Yitzhok Bashevis) did not cast himself as a humorist except when playing to a U.S. public. Coming of age in Poland at the height of Yiddish literary experimentation during and following World War I, he declared himself a devotee of realism, and made his reputation with stories and novels in a serious vein. Like many a nineteenth-century writer and like his older brother the Yiddish writer I. J. Singer, he published most of his long fiction in serial form, in the daily press. Fortunate to immigrate to New York in 1936, he was greatly affected by the disparity between his U.S. prospects and the fate of those he had left behind; the United States had freed him to the point of irrelevance while Europe was hunting down his fellow Jews in the cruelest search ever devised. To get across this scandalous contrast, he created images of imps who play around with human fate and the demonic writer who can do likewise with his characters.

The relatively innocent trickster of Yiddish joking becomes, in Singer's stories, the demon luring a bored young wife into one kind of sin and a coarsened butcher into another. Professional male and female liars are caught in their respective snares and destroy each other more completely than they could a naive victim of their trade. A final demon survives the destruction of the Jews, asking rhetorically, "Why demons, when man himself is a demon? Why persuade to evil someone who is already convinced?" Singer did not think that one could find a new kind of moral balance outside the code of Jewish law while doubting that modern man could "return" to the tradition's discipline.

The best known of Singer's stories, "Gimpel the Fool," translated by Saul Bellow in 1953, serves up this dilemma as if in the familiar Jewish comic tradition. Gimpel is the name of a Yiddish cartoon character, while the Hebrew word *tam*, Singer's term for fool, designates the simpleton among the Passover Haggadah's four sons and the "simple man" of Nahman of Bratslav's iconic story. We might also imagine the simpleton as the straight man of a burlesque team. Although the cuckold is a universal butt of comedy, none before Gimpel ever allowed himself to be married off to the town prostitute, or was ever complicit in his wife's adultery to the point of "siring" and raising six children, none of who proves to be his own. The laughingstock of the town, he remains trusting because he worries lest doubting his wife may lead to doubting God. The posture of faith is indistinguishable from gullibility.

Gimpel is not without his comic resources. When the Spirit of Evil comes to tempt him and asks, "Why do you sleep?" he replies, "What should I be doing? Eating *kreplach*?"[29] But once the story has milked this comedy, something in it seems to snap, moving it from comedy to another plane of fiction. Gimpel's unwarranted trust in others is credited with keeping him purer and happier than he would have been otherwise, and worthy of God's grace, if such were to be had. The joke, in other words, becomes a fable. Singer first mines the humor of his protagonist's excessive credulity, then shows its implications for a Yiddish-speaking Jewry that had just been massacred in Europe. His final sentence consigns the innocent to a heaven "where even Gimpel could not be deceived"—*or* where he learns that he has been the ultimate dupe.

Yiddish was inherently contradictory: a mongrel language to preserve Jewish distinctiveness, "secondary" language that became mother tongue, and in the modern period, vernacular that generated a world-class literature. Jews were a people exiled from a promised land and the chosen people of an elusive God. They were untroubled by such contradictions. They *required* forms of speech that incorporated incongruity and sought out expressions that bordered on absurdity. They epitomized the betrayal of good in a world of evil—and for that reason, if no other, Yiddish humor knew that it dared not succumb to the weight of evidence militating against its very existence.

Ultimately, however, even Sholem Aleichem could not always bear that weight. He admits as much in "The Haunted Tailor," which retells a familiar story about a hapless teacher of Chelm who is sent by his wife to a nearby town to purchase a goat so that their starving children may have some milk and returns instead with a billy goat—never having noticed the difference. (In alternate versions of the story, the goat's milk is required to heal the ailing rabbi.) The legendary Jewish fools' town of Chelm—on par with Britain's Gotham or Germany's Schilda—is noted for unworldly scholars and rabbis who habitually propose absurd solutions to straightforward problems as well as manifest hopeless innocence in the face of evil. In all these ways the story recorded as "The Chelm Goat Mystery" was typical of the genre.[30]

In Sholem Aleichem's version, the poor man is a patchwork tailor from the fictional town of Zolodievke, Shimen-Eli by name, an otherwise-ordinary soul with a slightly inflated sense of his own importance along with a liking for drink that prompts him to stop at a wayside tavern on both the outward and homeward legs of his journey. His mission accomplished, Shimen-Eli boasts of his purchase to the innkeeper, a rogue who surreptitiously substitutes a male goat for the milking animal. Naturally, the incensed wife berates her schlemiel husband and sends him back to correct his folly, but also naturally, he stops again at the inn, where the innkeeper once again exchanges the animals so that the original seller is able to milk the nanny goat and send Shimen-Eli back home with his original purchase. As in the Chelm folktale, the tailor walks through the same process a second time, and Maskilic criticism has no better target than this Jew who repeats the patterns of his life without investigating their causality.

But a joke stops being funny at the point that its consequence becomes fatal. Whereas the folktale ends with the rabbi's pronouncement, "Such is the luck of Chelm that by the time a nanny goat finally reaches our town, it's sure to turn

Russian Jewish artist Anatoli Kaplan (1902–80) created lithographic editions of a number of works by Sholem Aleichem, including "The Haunted Tailor." In this image, the tailor's wife berates her husband for bringing home a goat of the wrong gender: "That is a nanny goat as I am a rabbi's wife!" The children join in the mockery. The neofolk style of illustration is characteristic of Kaplan's interpretation of Sholem Aleichem.

into a billy!" Sholem Aleichem's version does not stop with this outcome. A local council of rabbis takes up the tailor's cause with its counterpart in the neighboring city; local craftspeople do the same and come to blows. But Shimen-Eli himself becomes convinced that the goat is a transmigrated soul of some dead antagonist, goes mad, and dies. The goat skips away scot-free. Sholem Aleichem concludes:

> "What is the moral of this tale?" the reader will ask. Don't press me, friends. It was not a good ending. The tale began cheerfully enough, and it ended as most such happy stories do—badly. And since you know the author of the story—that he is not naturally a gloomy fellow and hates to complain . . . then let the maker of the tale take his leave of you smiling, and let him wish you, Jews—and all mankind—more laughter than tears. Laughter is good for you. Doctors prescribe laughter.[31]

This tagline, on its own, would come to serve as a plug for the palliative benefits of Jewish humor. But as I observed in the introduction, prescribing doctors must constantly be mindful of the dangers of overdose. The careful reader of this tale cannot help noting that in it, Sholem Aleichem issues a powerful warning against just those dangers.

■ For their twenty-fifth wedding anniversary, Montreal friends of ours decided to entertain friends who knew Yiddish with readings from Sholem Aleichem by a local Yiddish actor. We gathered eagerly in the improvised comedy club. The actor had chosen a funny story and performed it well, but there was less and less laughter with every sentence. The humor was simply too dense—too intimate, too *good.* Rather than continuing with the second Sholem Aleichem story, our entertainer switched to a sketch by the American Yiddish humorist Moishe (Mark) Nudelman (1905–67)—a tale that was thinner in substance and heavily doused with English. This went off much better, inadvertently showing us how much was gone from our culture as opposed to how much of its richness had been retained. As though he had foreseen this, Sholem Aleichem's last will and testament instructed his family to gather for the anniversary of his death, his *yortsayt,* and read from his work in whatever language they understood.

Sholem Aleichem's influence on Yiddish was so strong that his language was mistaken for humorous in its essence. But though New York Jews may have accorded him the city's largest-ever funeral when he died there on May 13, 1916, his Yiddish writings never did go over big in the United States. The advent of hybrid Yinglish, like Spanglish, made it harder to appreciate intricate humor. In order to win new laughs from new audiences, Sholem Aleichem adaptations like *Fiddler on the Roof*—the musical version of his stories of Tevye the Dairyman—are obliged to alter at least as much as they retain.

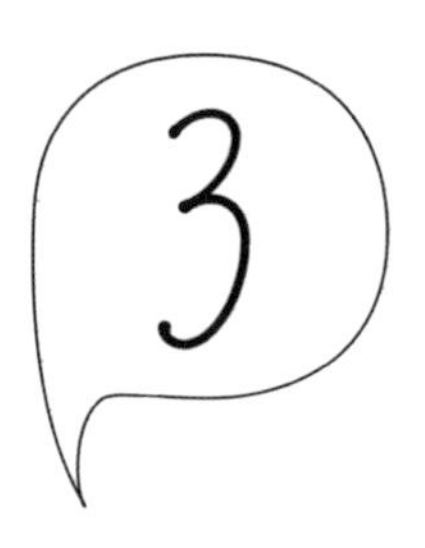

The Anglosphere

Let me entertain you
Let me make you smile

—From the musical *Gypsy*[1]

When and under what circumstances did Jewish humor become a marketable commodity, leaving the synagogue and Jewish study-house to take the public stage?

With their entry into European society, Jews began making their mark in the arts; we have seen how writers like Heine and Kafka exploited the doubled perspective of outsider-insiders and insider-outsiders for comedy. This chapter charts a further step: namely, the penetration of non-Jewish society, first in England and then in the United States, by Jewish humor and Jewish humorists—to the point where, by 1975, an estimated three-quarters of U.S. comedy professionals, from Woody Allen to Henny Youngman, were Jewish. Moreover, much (though not all) of their comedy was itself perceptibly Jewish in its references and style.

Jews had traditionally earned their keep in host societies by supplying necessary services and goods. How did they create a demand for Jewish joking?

That they had often been the *targets* of humor is not surprising, given their long-standing political dependency and the delight taken by satirists in ridiculing alleged inferiors. The Roman writer Juvenal lampooned the Jews' squatting and sponging; his compatriots derided their religious credulity; even the generally sympathetic fourth-century emperor Flavius Claudius Julianus (Julian the Apostate) taunted their weakness:

> But now answer me this: Is it better to be free continuously and during two-thousand whole years to rule over the greater part of the earth and the sea, or to be enslaved and to live in obedience to the will of others? No man is so lacking in self-respect as to choose the latter in preference. Again, will anyone think that victory in war is less desirable than defeat? Who is so stupid?[2]

One can see Julian's point. Jews prided themselves on being the people chosen by God, "Lord of Hosts," yet they boasted not a single general of the stature of Alexander or Caesar. The discrepancy between Jewish claims of election and their unhappy experience in other people's lands provoked many sallies of this kind at their expense, from Geoffrey Chaucer to Louis-Ferdinand Céline and many in between. All too many Western writers enjoyed ridiculing the Jews.

Nor is it surprising that among themselves, Jews should have encouraged some merriment alongside their rituals of mourning. In the previous chapter I highlighted the ritualized cheer on the holiday of Purim, mandated by the Book of Esther with its portrait of a clumsy king and tale of triumphant political reversal. Many Jewish communities traditionally celebrated Purim as a funfest of inversions; over time, they cultivated entertainers like the Purim rabbi, wedding joker, and other roguish wits. But all these were strictly for internal consumption. The question, again, is at what point Jews undertook to turn their own brands of humor to the task of amusing their fellow citizens.

I think the answer lies in the very concept of fellow citizens. The *profession* of Jewish comedy arose in societies where legal barriers separating Jews from their neighbors were leveled, but without necessarily establishing instantaneous trust between them. Liberal democracy invites free expression, including of the discomfiting sort. Already targets of mockery and adept at self-mockery, Jews had only to forge a new combination of the two for the titillation of a general audience that could, perhaps nervously, laugh along with those whom it did not yet fully trust. The process then proceeded apace: once liberal culture began ascribing a positive value to a sense of humor and comedy became king, the toleration of humor was overtaken by the expectation of humor, and Jews rushed in where they could earn their bread.

■ One of the first to exploit the potential of Jewish comedy for an emerging liberal public was Israel Zangwill (1864–1926). Born in London to Jewish immigrants (his father was from Russia, and his mother was from Poland), Zangwill became a bar mitzvah in 1877, a year after the appearance of George Eliot's *Daniel Deronda*—a book that both charted and quickened Britain's removal of social barriers against Jews and Judaism. In this last of her novels, Eliot replaced the prevailing demand of full assimilation and Anglicization with a different ideal, which would come to be known as Zionism. Her hero discovers that he is a Jew, and that he wants to remain one, marry a Jewish woman, and help reclaim the land of his ancestors. So, too, Zangwill discovered that conversion to Christianity was no longer required as a ticket of admission to British culture and became for a time a British Zionist. In his fiction, inventing or perfecting a brand of integrationist humor that accorded well with the genteel satire of his milieu, Zangwill contributed to debates over what it meant to be an Englishman *and* a Jew.

No one could have hoped to displace Shakespeare's Shylock as the most memorable Jew in British literature, or in Charles Dickens's *Oliver Twist*, the despicable Fagin, who trains boys in the arts of stealing and deception. One way or another, as bankroller or pawnbroker, the shyster Jew of English literature would always be present in the British imagination, scheming to "jew" cultivated Christians out of their innocence and cash. Rather than fight this stereotype, Zangwill's 1894 comic masterwork *King of the Schnorrers* turns it inside out, inviting the British to enjoy what they had reviled and feared. So you think Jews care only for money and contrive to get it by nefarious means? That they use their cleverness to exploit others without ever earning an "honest" penny through hard work? Very well (Zangwill seems to be saying), I will show you how charmingly they get it done—*and* in the process, how similar their scams are to ones practiced in the higher reaches of British society.

King of the Schnorrers transposes the repertoire of schnorrer joking into a British milieu. Shylock's hauteur doesn't hold a candle to that of Manassah Bueno Bazillai Azavedo da Costa, every syllable of whose name recalls a Spanish Jewish ancestry that (at least in fiction) puts him atop the pecking order of British Jews. Indeed, refugees from the Inquisition in Spain and Portugal at the end of the fifteenth century had been the first Jews to "return" to Britain after the community's expulsion by the edict of Edward I in 1290. They were followed by German Jews, fleeing persecution in central Europe, and lastly by the Russian immigrants who were pouring into England in Zangwill's time. In this hierarchy of first arrivals, the impecunious da Costa lords it over his nouveau riche German Jewish compatriot Joseph Grobstock (thick stick), while both of them outrank the Polish newcomer Yankele, who wants to marry da Costa's daughter. Collectively, the three Jews—da Costa the fallen "nobleman," Grobstock the insecure bourgeois, and Yankele the penniless invader—parody their British equivalents in, respectively, the aristocratic, moneyed, and working class.

To put readers at their ease, Zangwill situates his comic novel a century earlier, when Jews suffered from British liabilities that had since been overcome.

> In the days when Lord George Gordon became a Jew, and was suspected of insanity; when, out of respect for the prophecies, England denied her Jews every civic right except that of paying taxes; when the *Gentleman's Magazine* had ill words for the infidel alien; when Jewish

> marriages were invalid and bequests for Hebrew colleges void; when a prophet prophesying Primrose Day would have been set in the stocks, though [William] Pitt inclined his private ear to Benjamin Goldsmid's views on the foreign loans—in those days, when Tevele Schiff was Rabbi in Israel, and Dr. de Falk, the Master of the Tetragrammaton, saint and Cabbalistic conjuror, flourished in Wellclose Square, and the composer of "The Death of Nelson" was a choir-boy in the Great Synagogue, Joseph Grobstock, pillar of the same, emerged one afternoon into the spring sunshine at the fag-end of the departing stream of worshippers. In his hand was a large canvas bag, and in his eye a twinkle.[3]

The chain of clauses in this opening paragraph of Zangwill's novel recalls a time of prejudice and discrimination, or a period when British hypocrisy limited competition from those whose wealth it exploited. The historical drumroll stops at Grobstock emerging from a synagogue service that happens to be honoring a British monarch: "The congregation was large and fashionable—far more so than when only a heavenly sovereign was concerned."[4]

We come on Grobstock in the act of distributing coins of various denominations in a lottery system of his own devising. As Grobstock tries to make a kind of game of his charity, the ostentatiously shabby da Costa exposes his philanthropy as no more than self-indulgence. (Indeed, superficial do-gooderism was then coming under fire in Britain as a disguised form of do-nothingism.) Contriving to have himself invited for a sabbath meal, and promised a gift of Grobstock's cast-off clothing so that Mrs. Grobstock will not know they have a beggar at their table, da Costa begins to treat it as his own while it is still on its owner's back. "Take care, you are sputtering sauce all over that waistcoat, without any consideration for me."[5]

Manassah and his Polish sidekick Yankele examine a theater poster of a London play they then see from box seats—without purchasing tickets. Drawings by George Hutchinson accompany almost all editions of *King of the Schnorrers*, which has been in print since 1894.

Nor does he then deign to wear the clothes he is given, selling them instead to a secondhand dealer.

"Why did you sell my clothes?" Grobstock asks, insulted by the beggar's disdain for his own finer attire. "You did not expect me to wear them?" da Costa replies. "No, I know my station, thank God." Thus does the king of the schnorrers deliver a stunningly aggressive rebuke to the man who has tried to ingratiate himself with his alleged betters and ends by trembling before the judgment of his inferior.

Here it is worth contrasting Zangwill with Heine when it comes to portraying Jews making their unorthodox way in a Gentile world. Whereas the German poet presents the Jew as a bewitched canine who gets to feel human only once a week, Zangwill's Jew has never lost his regal bearing. Unlike Gumpelino and Hirsch-Hyacinth, who have traded in their names to climb the social ladder, da Costa flaunts every feature of his Jewish inheritance. The more expertly he works the system, the more we relish his challenge to its hypocrisies and abuses, and such conventions as working for a living or abiding by local institutional rules. It is the essential benignity of British society, despite its prejudices, that establishes the gentler tone of this social satire in which the worst thing one suffers is loss of dignity.

Social satire happened to be a highly developed form of British writing by the time Zangwill joined its ranks. Relatively good-natured, and in some respects reminiscent of P. G. Wodehouse's later jabs at the British upper-class establishment in the novels featuring the aristocratic fop Bertie Wooster and his manservant Jeeves, Zangwill's comedy in the end rewards even poor Grobstock for the natural sympathies he has shown throughout. Da Costa pulls off a "royal wedding" for his daughter and the upstart Yankele, enriches the Spanish synagogue that he bilked to pay for the nuptials, and has Grobstock invest the money to secure the future of them both—proving the advantages of his way of life and good it can bring to others. If we accept the schnorrer as a stand-in for the Jew—compensating for his social liability through elevated self-esteem—da Costa proves the advantages of his principled way of life, and perhaps also the advantages of Jewish humor that comes at its own expense and not at someone else's.

Zangwill was no Dickens, but his scroungers are undeniably funnier than Fagin. They take only what is given them—however grudgingly; they keep their word, if sometimes altering its spirit; they stay true to the principles of their profession of schnorring, different as it may be from other professions; they display the dignity of the righteous without the conceit of the self-righteous; and they never overtly make fun of goyim. In sum, they defy the stereotype of the grasping Jew that they also embody, inviting laughter at themselves along with their victims. At the same time, Gentiles may feel an extra bit of satisfaction at being *invited* to laugh at what would seem to be negative Jewish stereotypes.

All this coincides with what the British humorist Stephen Potter describes as a shift in British humor away from "self-congratulation and even sadism of laughing at, to the sympathy and even compassion of laughing with."[6] It was not to last. Fourteen years after writing *King of the Schnorrers*, Zangwill, who had by then happily married a Gentile woman and was in a different frame of mind regarding the future of the Jews as a people proudly apart, wrote *The Melting Pot*, a tendentious play situated in the United States that promotes assimilation as a U.S. ideal. We may see this as an element of an overall move away from Jewish subjects and entry into a more exclusively English literary milieu, and away from comedy at a time when the "great age of British humour" was itself coming to an end.[7] The First World War crushed the good-natured British satire of 1894, and Zangwill's brand of Jewish humor followed the British trend—although I will have occasion later on to point out certain continuities as well.

■ The evolution portrayed by Potter, from *laughing at* to *laughing with*, is wonderfully illustrated by Richard Raskin in his study of classic Jewish jokes, one of which he traces back to an anecdote recorded in a London publication of 1822:

> On one of the nights when Mrs. Siddons first performed at the Drury Lane, a Jew boy, in his eagerness to get to the first row in the shilling gallery, fell over into the pit, and was dangerously hurt. The managers of the theatre ordered the lad to be conveyed to a lodging, and he was attended by their own physician; but notwithstanding all their attention, he died, and was decently buried at the expense of the theatre. The mother came to the playhouse to thank the managers, and they gave her his clothes and five guineas, for which she returned a curtsy, but with some hesitation added [that] they had forgotten to return her the shilling which Abraham had paid for coming in.[8]

Whether or not we choose to label this joke anti-Semitic, its sympathy obviously flows toward the exemplary Gentiles and against the mother, grasping even in her bereavement. The joke turns on her unexpected substitution of an insignificant sum for the so much more serious loss she has incurred. Raskin then traces the evolution of the joke through several variants before arriving at what, for its fusion of the practical, psychological, and metaphysical, he considers "one of the finest Jewish jokes we have today":

> Mrs. Markowitz was walking along the beach with her grandson when suddenly a wave came and washed the three-year-old boy out to sea.
>
> "Oh Lord!" cried the woman. "If you'll just bring that boy back alive I'll do anything. I'll be the best person. I'll give to charity. I'll go to temple. Please, God! Send him back!"
>
> At that moment, a wave washed the child back up on the sand, safe and sound. His grandmother looked at the boy and then up to the heavens.
>
> "Okay!" she exclaimed. "So where's his hat?"

The focus of the original anecdote has shifted away from behavioral differences between Jews and Christians to alleged qualities of the Jew, which Raskin summarizes thus: "[No] one can satisfy a Jewish mother, not even God producing a miracle in compliance with her most desperate prayer."[9] The grandmother still bears traces of the anti-Jewish cast in which she was conceived, but what figured earlier as greed now places her in the tradition of Jewish God arguers from the patriarch

Abraham to Rabbi Levi Yitzhok of Berdichev, affectionately known as the "defense attorney of the Jewish people." The joke denies us the relief of a child's rescue by switching its attention to a preposterously exaggerated demand for perfect justice from the perfect judge. The no-nonsense Jew is the insatiably demanding Jew is the Jew who intends to hold God to His promise.

What Raskin omits to tell us in his otherwise-exhaustive treatment of this joke's evolution is that its later, "metaphysical" versions emerged not in England but rather in the United States. In its U.S. versions, the joke includes no juxtaposition of Jews with Gentiles. Instead, it plays off warring elements in the Jewish psyche itself, and in a way that the American Saul Bellow defines as "characteristically Jewish." In narratives of this type, according to the novelist,

> laughter and trembling are so curiously mingled that it is not easy to determine the relations of the two. At times the laughter seems simply to restore the equilibrium of sanity; at times the figures of the story, or parable, appear to invite or encourage trembling with the secret aim of overcoming it by means of laughter.

Bellow thinks that when we laugh, our minds refer us to God's existence. He emphasizes that "chaos is *exposed*."[10] One might reverse this remotely Hasidic concept so as to suggest that the best of Jewish humor recalls the improbable contract that earthly Jews entered into with the Ineffable, saying (Exodus 24:7), "We will do and we will hearken"—in that counter-intuitive order. If Jewish humor exposes chaos, it exposes no less an unwillingness to *make do* with chaos, pitting people's expectations of God against God's of human beings, with no way of guaranteeing the outcome.

Illustrating Bellow's thesis even better than the Mrs. Markowitz joke is one that he adduces from his own repertoire. This joke is about three Jews boasting of their rabbis:

> One said, "My rabbi's faith is so great and he fears the Lord so much that he trembles day and night, and he has to be belted into his bed at night with straps so that he doesn't fall out." The second said, "Yes, you have a marvelous rabbi, but he really can't be compared to my rabbi. Mine is so holy and so just that he makes God tremble. God is afraid of displeasing him. And if the world has not been going so well lately, you can figure it out for yourselves. God is trembling." The third Jew said, "Your rabbis are both great men. No doubt about it. But my rabbi passed through both stages. For a long time he trembled, too, and in the second stage, he made God tremble. But then he thought it over very carefully and finally he said to God, 'Look—why should we both tremble?' "[11]

The final question, cunningly phrased as a gesture of conciliation, undermines the pious claims entered by the other two boasters by establishing human beings as God's equal rather than His subjects. The wisecrack remains just this side of heresy, retaining the language of awe while upending its premise of a divine-human divide. And although Bellow offers no comment on the joke, his definition of what is characteristically Jewish deflates not only the devoutness of pietists but also the very concept of "fear and trembling"—a favorite of certain twentieth-century students of religion drawn to the thought and in this case the phraseology of the Danish theologian Søren Aabye Kierkegaard. In the end, Bellow makes the analysis of humor almost as funny as the humor itself.

■ The open, much more freely competitive culture of the United States produced more so-called characteristically Jewish brands of humor than the social satire of England—though not all at once. The 1940s introduced two complementary perceptions of the Jews that greatly eased their acceptance. The greatest boon to the comfortable integration of Jews in the United States was the creation in 1948 of the state of Israel. Not only did the old-new homeland of the Jewish people come to serve as the "Mother of Exiles" for Jewish refugees from Europe and Arab lands who might otherwise have flooded the U.S. shores; the perception of Jews as a people taking hold of their future also appealed to Americans who valued a similar capacity for pulling themselves up by their own bootstraps.

At the same time, the genocide that generated those new refugees awakened the sympathy of their U.S. rescuers. Leon Uris's 1958 best-selling novel *Exodus* captured the budding U.S. love affair with the Jewish state—a state that needed no help from the United States in repelling British overseers and Arab attackers alike. In the novel, the all-American Kitty Fremont overcomes her dislike of Jews through simultaneous admiration for a tough-minded Israeli warrior and compassion for a European child survivor. She wants to marry the one and adopt the other.

This new U.S. forbearance occurred, finally, on the cusp of a broad civil rights movement that in striving to erase the legacy of slavery, also vastly broadened interest in "foreign cultures" and made a value of ethnic self-expression. The distinctively Jewish humor that emerged in the United States during this era was a by-product of a greater Jewish self-confidence that was itself part of the spirit of the 1960s.

But I am getting ahead of myself. Until the end of the Second World War, the United States was not much more comfortable than Great Britain with the religious and national distinctiveness of Jews. From the 1920s through the 1940s, Jewish entertainers served the general public largely with Christmas music, films about marriage to Christian women, and joking. "I don't want to join any club that would have me as a member," said Groucho Marx, lampooning the Jew in himself who disdains the welcome of his own kind in favor of the restrictions placed on him by others. Since the presumptive appeal of Groucho's joke is proportional to one's discomfort with one's identity, it bears noting that this became his most famous line.

Zangwill's closest U.S. counterpart during the early, strained period of Americanization was Leo Rosten (1908–97), who happened to be something of an Anglophile, just as Zangwill was something of an adopted American. Born in Poland, raised in Chicago in a Yiddish-speaking family, and a graduate of the London School of Economics and University of Chicago, Rosten seemed headed for a career in the social sciences when he sold a comic sketch to the *New Yorker* based on a job he had briefly held teaching English in a night school. Expanded into *The Education of H*Y*M*A*N K*A*P*L*A*N*

(1937), the work was published under the pseudonym Leonard Q. Ross, allegedly because the author did not want his professors to discover that he was writing humor, though the name's Gentile ring suggests a slightly different explanation.

The book's plot was simple: Mr. Parkhill, a teacher of exemplary patience, instructs a collection of immigrants in English. Most of the students are Jews (along with a Pole and Greek as well as a Mrs. Rodriguez and Mrs. Tomasic), and most are slow. The exceptions are the conscientious spinster Rose Mitnick and irrepressible Kaplan, the "star" of the class who compensates through invention for what he lacks in mastery. Kaplan (the asterisks in his name are his) is as ebullient as Zangwill's da Costa was aggressive and no less threatening to the (linguistic) status quo.

Some of Rosten's comic method can be deduced from his admiration for Groucho—"the man from Marx"—whose wit he considered "a form of surrealism."[12] Rosten appreciated the master comic's "singular faculty of *hearing* with originality," which allowed him to ambush the unwary word. But whereas early in his career Groucho left ambiguous the ethnicity of his comic persona, Rosten made Jews his most ostentatious greenhorns and showed how resourcefully they in particular could mangle the language. Let us count the veys. Through logical induction: if the feminine of the word host is hostess, then the feminine of the word ghost must be ghostess; in the same way, the conjugation of write, wrote, and written corresponds to bite, bote, and bitten. Via creative mishearing: Mary had a little lamb whose fleas were white as snow; the waterway that connects the Atlantic and Pacific is the Panama

Kennel. Through inventive grammar: for the positive word bad, its comparative would be the term worse, and its superlative would be the word rotten. And through original etymology: Montana was so named because it is full of mountains; Ohio sounds like an Indian yawning.

Mr. Parkhill's function is to teach proper English, and Kaplan's to reinvent it. "Mr. Kaplan had a way of getting Mr. Parkhill to submit each rule to the test of reason, and Mr. Parkhill was beginning to face the awful suspicion that he was no match for Mr. Kaplan, who had a way of operating with rules of reason entirely his own."[13] Mitnick is likewise humbled by her rival. Always correcting, she gloats when she catches the sentence in Kaplan's exercise letter to his uncle, "If your *eye* falls on a bargain pick *it* up." The class bursts into laughter, and even Mr. Parkhill "permitted himself a dignified smile." Kaplan smiles as well, with self-assurance that anticipates a wondrous reversal: " 'Mine oncle,' he said, 'has a gless eye.' "[14] Kaplan is seldom this vaudevillian, but Rosten never deviates from the same formula that Zangwill applied in having the most "impaired" speaker of English carry the day.

Kaplan proves his patriotism in spectacular displays of individuality that turn his failures into triumph. His apparent inability to master the host language actually demonstrates a U.S. kind of ingenuity, as mistakes become new ways of appreciating the elasticity and inventiveness of English. Yet although Kaplan's Jewishness is taken for granted, the only explicit reference to anything Jewish is the mention of Hanukkah in a class discussion of Christmas. Jewishness may be the implicit basis of the comedy, but the Gentile reader is never confronted with any particularity that suggests Judaism's meaningful distinctiveness or might impede an appreciation of the humor.

Whereas Zangwill over the course of his literary life gradually distanced himself from his Jewish immigrant origins, Rosten followed an opposite trajectory. His 1960s *The Joys of Yiddish* and its sequel *The Joys of Yinglish* appeared under the Rosten name, which itself became a trademark for salable, specifically Jewish humor. By "joys," Rosten means the comic potential of Yiddish, which he presents as an essentially comical language:

> A woman, feeling sorry for a beggar who had come to her door, invited him in and offered him food. On the table was a pile of dark bread—and a few slices of *hallah*. The shnorrer promptly fell upon the *hallah*.
>
> "There's black bread, too," the woman hinted.
>
> "I prefer *hallah*."
>
> "But *hallah* is much more expensive!"
>
> "Lady," said the beggar, "it's worth it."[15]

The joke (of which there are many versions) serves as Rosten's elucidation of chutzpah, "gall, brazen nerve, effrontery, incredible 'guts'; presumption-plus-arrogance such as no other word, and no other language, can do justice to." In fact, a better illustration of chutzpah might be Rosten himself, who as Ross turned a Yiddish accent into a joke and who as Rosten, with the change of U.S. fashion, then turned the Jewish language into a laughing matter.

The most important single factor in the professionalization of Jewish humor in the United States would have to be the Borscht Belt. Named for the beet soup that was popular among Jews (and other eastern Europeans), the string of Jewish-owned hotels in the Catskill Mountains of New York State provided comedy as one of the main attractions. In their heyday, these hotels employed most of the Jewish comedians in the country, performing (in the estimation of one historian) over six hundred shows on a typical Saturday night.[16]

Freddy Roman (Kirschenbaum), lifetime "dean" of the New York Friars' Club, got his start as emcee in the Crystal Spring Hotel owned by his uncle and grandfather. As he has described the Borscht Belt's culture of comedy, the hotel staff, including the waiters, waiters' assistants, and pool attendants, were expected to amuse the guests as part of their service. Comic games of "Simon says" took precedence over nature walks, as did the "social director" over the swimming instructor. *Tummlers*, from the Yiddish *tuml* for "noise," were expected to keep guests' minds off their troubles, and deflect complaints over food and accommodations. The term tummler recalls the antics of the comedian Jerry Lewis (Joseph Levitch), who developed a routine featuring a bumptious waiter always spilling the trays—an act that reportedly originated while Lewis was a waiter in a Jewish hotel.

One-liners were standard fare:

> What are the three words a woman doesn't want to hear when she's making love?
>
> "Honey, I'm home."

A recent Wikipedia list of those who got their start in these hotels includes (under "B" alone) Milton Berle (Berlinger), Joey Bishop (Joseph Abraham Gottlieb), Mel Brooks (Melvin Kaminsky), Lenny Bruce (Schneider), George Burns (Nathan Birnbaum), and Red Buttons (Aaron Chwatt). Economic incentive brought together hotelkeepers who were trying to retain a skittish clientele, entrepreneurial young men trying to earn some "easy" money (easier than running a hotel), and Jews looking for escape from the cities where making a living was synonymous with living. But once the new business got under way, it was as competitive as any other, with would-be comedians stealing lines from other performers who sold exclusive rights to their repertoires to as many as would buy them. Joey Adams (Joseph Abramowitz) describes spending "three days without food or water" transcribing George Jessel's trademark telephone routine with his "mother":

> "Mama, how do you like the lovebird I bought for the front room? . . . You cooked it? . . . You cooked a South American bird? A bird that speaks three languages?—Oh, you didn't know[?] . . . He should have said something!"

Mining this motif for comedy, Adams complains that the social director at a certain hotel had lifted the original gags that Adams himself had bought from his fellow comic Lou Saxon, who had stolen the jokes from the "gag fence" Eddie Davis, who had received them from Leon Fields, who had gotten them from Buddy Walker, who had copied them down from Berle "at Loew's State [theater] when they were still warm."[17]

A good joke became worth its weight in gold. Although a comedian could not make the big time without developing a distinctive stage personality, the profession itself became more streamlined, with teams of writers stockpiling and market-testing material, agents packaging performers for emerging markets, and union protection securing the comedians' old age. The sociology of the Borscht Belt ensured that most of the humorists, like most of the guests, would be Jewish. When the emerging medium of radio went looking for entertainers, it took those who had mastered timing and delivery. Movies and television picked off talent from the stage and radio. Jews developed comedy the way Chinese restaurants taught the United States to eat with chopsticks.

In a "roast" of Frank Sinatra—the lampooning of a fellow comedian in the company of other comedians having become itself a strategy for promoting the profession—Buttons observed that in the entertainment industry, most singers were Italians and most comedians Jewish, "which is ridiculous: very little difference between the Jews and Italians. One year of high school."[18] But the phenomenon does raise the question, How come Jewish hotelkeepers in the Catskills turned comedy into a main attraction?

Gentile hotels in the Adirondacks advertised no such specialty; nor did the first Jewish resorts in the period before and immediately after the First World War. In one such hotel described by Abraham Cahan in his 1917 novel *The Rise of David Levinsky*, the entertainment consists of high-minded patriotic fare. Summer colonies for Jewish socialists and union workers offered lectures by prominent Yiddish writers, poets, and thinkers, who sought to enlighten more than to amuse. Even Nadir, one of the best Yiddish humorists (as we saw in the previous chapter), did not make comedy a main attraction at the summer resort he ran in the 1920s. It wasn't until Jews began to feel a touch more comfortable in the United States that they adopted laughter as their main collective pursuit, along with the fund-raising that was sometimes its accompaniment. "A man is hit by a car. A paramedic on the scene asks, 'Are you comfortable?' The Jew answers [with a Yiddish accent], 'I make a living.'" What funnier to a crowd of by-now middle-income vacationers than a joke by a fellow Jew with a Yiddish, Yinglish, or Yiddish-accented punch line that confirms how far they have come, both economically and linguistically? What more reassuring than the collective laughter at a joke that "no one but a Jew" could understand?

For a time, in the early decades of the twentieth century, Yiddish theater had served as a quasisynagogue—a spiritual sanctuary and cultural gathering place. Although secular in nature, performed on Friday nights, and often dramatizing the defiance of religious norms, the typical Yiddish play featured one or more ritual scenes—celebrations of a holiday, engagement, or wedding, circumcision, or sabbath—as though to make up for the ceremonial occasions that the audience was no longer observing at home. Yiddish theater was intensely interactive, like performances in the Elizabethan theater, eliciting tears and laughter along with outbursts of approval or displeasure. Habits of collective participation did not carry over, however, to the English-language stage. Meshulim Meier Weisenfreund might find personal fame as the actor Paul

Muni, and some Jewish stories might transport well to Broadway and Hollywood, but at non-Jewish performances, Jewish audiences behaved decorously.

Appropriate in this connection is the joke, originating in Yiddish and already related in the previous chapter, about the Jewish widow who conscientiously studies proper Gentile dress, speech, and demeanor, and when she feels ready to "pass," registers at a restricted hotel. She is doing well until the waiter who is bringing the "dry martini" she has ordered accidentally spills it into her lap, causing her to yelp, "Oy vey!—whatever *that* means!" In its U.S. (as opposed to European) context, the joke implies: Why go to a Gentile hotel when you can laugh with us here in the Catskills?!

In brief, the kind of participatory audience reaction once elicited by the Yiddish theater found its home in the comedy shows of Jewish hotels. The Borsht Belt became to stand-up comedy what New Orleans was to jazz—an incubator of a new form of entertainment that gradually emerged from its formative center into the U.S. mainstream and beyond.

Not that this comparison of Jewish comedy with jazz should obscure the contributions of Jews to the development of jazz itself, or black Americans to the growth of native comedy. The two forms of entertainment were similarly informal and improvisational. But the value placed by each community on its special cultural pastime dictated the opportunities for talented individuals within that community. Comedy and jazz depend on patronage, which rewards what it craves. Jews wanted to laugh at their failings, and they rewarded the comics who mocked their flaws just as they had once prized the authorities and rabbinic tradition that had tried to make them more perfect. Jewish stand-up comedians took over from the *maggidim*—the preachers who punished and promised redemption—the function of reprimand, without which Jews would cease to be Jews.

In some crucial respects, Catskills comedy differed profoundly from New Orleans jazz: while southern blacks were still suffering exclusion, the vacationing Jews were anxiously protecting their advancement in U.S. society. Though much can be made of the anti-Semitism that was on the rise in the United States during the 1930s—instituting restrictions and quotas even where none had been present before—Jews were creating clubs of their own with patrons who valued their intimacy. The majority of Jews would have reversed Groucho's dictum to read, "I would never join a club that didn't want me for a member."

Yet the good fortune that now allowed them to vacation in the Catskills was as incongruous as the punch lines of some of the jokes. More than anti-Semitism directed at *Jews*, U.S. isolationism threatened to abandon the Jewish people elsewhere to their fate at the hands of determined enemies. A growing disparity separated American Jews, whose security was increasing in every meaningful respect, from the Jews of Europe and Palestine, the former threatened by Hitler and Stalin, and the latter sustaining increased Arab violence under British rule. The Yiddish press agitated on behalf of these fellow Jews, but most English-language media discouraged intervention. For their part, resort hotels were expected to insulate vacationers from their worries.

What, then, are we to make of the fantastic spurt of Jewish laughter in the very years when American Jews ought, perhaps, to have been laughing less and doing more?

■ As it happens, my experience at a Catskill resort in winter 1974 enlarged my sympathy for the apparently inappropriate causes and effects of comedy. My beloved older brother Benjamin, before his death on November 25 of that year, had arranged for an elaborate winter holiday with his wife and three children. We did not know what to do with ourselves after the week of shivah, much less how to console his widow and children. Our closest friend, a rabbi's daughter, suggested that after the month of mourning we all go to Grossinger's, queen of the Catskill hotels: she with her husband and their four children, we with our three, and my widowed sister-in-law with hers. Basing herself on her kibbutz experience, our friend laid out the advantages of being together at this sprawling resort with meals and activities provided, abler to attend to the children and our grief.

Evenings proved harder than days. Though it seemed a desecration, the older children and we attended the comedy shows that were the resort's prime distraction, and the comedy began to suit our mood. There was the routine about a bar mitzvah party that keeps getting more and more elaborate until the candles on the cake set off the sprinkler system that floods the place. The nervously pacing stand-up comic was not unlike my brother, which made me laugh, which was not that different from crying. Laughter brought on tears that became independent of the comedy triggering them, and left me purged in their aftermath. Comedy complicated the physiological and psychological relation between shaking and shuddering in ways that I could not have anticipated.

Stand-up comedy is all about nerve—a battle between aggressor and victims with wit as the weapon and laughter as the prize. Different from prizefights that pit people against one another in the presence of paying spectators, comedy pits the fighter against the paying customers, with silence as the killer, and the detonation of laughter as the victory. As in any pitched battle, tension is at the heart of the matter, and the pent-up tension in those rooms full of Jews must have driven the value of comedy to record heights. In the 1930s, the political threat to Jews elsewhere belied the incremental prosperity of Jews in the United States, though the United States was itself still jeopardized by social and economic handicaps that were contrary to the promise of equality. Strength and helplessness, promise and danger, advantage and liability all had seldom, if ever, converged as incongruously as in the years when Jewish comedians were "makin' whoopee" (lyrics by Gus Kahn) in the mountains.

It therefore was not unreasonable for Jewish comedy to be directed inward, if not at the situation itself, then at reflected hints of it in habits of conspicuous consumption, overhasty Americanization, and men who could or would not manifest their masculinity. Henpecked husbands, sad sacks, and what Jews called nebbishes, schlimazels, and schlemiels emerged as trademarks of American Jewish comedy. In a later routine, Jackie Mason (Maza), scion of rabbis and himself an ordained rabbi, twits Jewish husbands who cannot order food without permission from their wives. "Do I like this? . . . I thought I did. . . . I don't? It's up to you." They can't walk around in the house for which they've paid a half-million dollars or drink from a glass because it is always the wrong one. They have to get permission from their wives even to laugh. Mason taunts the males who in their domestic arrangements replicate the stereotype of the homeless Jew. Joan Rivers (Molinsky Sanger Rosenberg) is equally caustic on the subject of the (Jewish) woman who does not satisfy her husband: heavy breathing from his side of the bed signals an attack of asthma. Woody Allen's take on the weak Jewish male would be contrastingly seductive, ridiculing Gentiles—American, Russian, and Christian—for their brawn and Western culture for its ideal of the bellicose hero; but his is the exception that underlines the rule.

From among the hundreds of professional Jewish comedians, there is no way of choosing the routines or personae that had the greatest or most lasting impact—whether the Three Stooges on absurdist theory, Gertrude Berg's Molly Goldberg as the cheerful good neighbor waving from her window, the exaggerated parsimony of Jack Benny (Benjamin Kubelsky), the exaggerated innocence of Danny Kaye (David Daniel Kaminsky), Lenny Bruce challenging the legal limits of profanity, Sid Caesar dominating *Your Show of Shows*, or Jerry Seinfeld and Larry David playing sharply contrasting versions of themselves. It does seem, however, that the socioeconomics of the Borscht Belt created the opportunity for a Jewish-style comedy less eager for Gentile approval than for exploring some of the mysteries of what Mason called the "Ultimate Jew."

The most cultic line in American Jewish comedy may have been uttered in the Coen Brothers' 1998 film *The Big Lebowski*. John Goodman plays Walter Sobchak, a convert to Judaism, formerly a Polish Catholic, who won't participate in the bowling league tournament because he is "shomer shabbos." "Saturday, Donny, is Shabbos, the Jewish day of rest. That means that I don't work, I don't drive a car, I don't fucking ride in a car, I don't handle money, I don't turn on the oven, and I sure as shit don't fucking roll!" This fiercely obscene and obscenely fierce defense of halachic observance draws a laugh all the louder because such words had never before been uttered in U.S. entertainment by any born Jew. Humor is all about incongruity, and integration in the United States had gone so far that a Polish Catholic—once a paradigm of the anti-Semite—could be portrayed as the conscience of his adopted religion. In this scene, it would be hard to separate laughing *at* the dysfunctional team of Jewish losers, improbable convert, and demands of Jewish observance from laughing *with* the same dysfunctional team of losers, improbable convert, and demands of Jewish observance. Yet Jews are the unquestionable insiders of this humor, and in humor it's the insider's edge that counts.

■ One or another version of the challenged Jewish male whom Allen tries to turn into a matinee idol has dominated not just stand-up comedy but also some of the best American Jewish writing, which also turns out to be—how surprising is that?—some of its funniest. A seemingly exasperated Bellow once referred to himself, Bernard Malamud, and Roth as the

"Hart Schaffner & Marx" of U.S. fiction. The allusion was to the Chicago Jewish firm that produced an upscale brand of men's suits, so that Bellow was staking a claim to a label of distinction while professedly complaining about being unfairly labeled. In Wallace Markfield's darkly hilarious *To an Early Grave* (1964), four Jewish writers end up at the wrong funeral. Jewish shopkeepers are the *Criers and Kibitzers, Kibitzers and Criers* of Stanley Elkin's comic stories (1966). A junior professor shows up with an open fly in Malamud's *A New Life* (1961). Bellow's Moses Herzog arranges a job for the best friend who is cuckolding him (1964). Bruce Jay Friedman's eponymous hero in *Stern* (1962), seeking calm in the suburbs, cultivates an ulcer instead. While one should not exaggerate the function of comedy in a body of literature that also features the tortured writing of Henry Roth in *Call It Sleep* (1934) or replicate the offense to Yiddish by turning literature into an "essentially comic" medium, neither can we ignore the fact that Joseph Heller's comic novel *Catch-22* (1961) gave American English its synonym for Kafkaesque. The decade ushered in by Heller's "Armenian" captain John Joseph Yossarian would end with Philip Roth's funniest novel, *Portnoy's Complaint* (1969).

Roth spoofs familiar and new constituencies in a *shpritz* so manic it might have been fueled by drugs, except that there has seldom been a writer as soberly concentrated as Roth on mastering the craft of fiction. *Portnoy's Complaint* was a breakthrough in the way that *The Adventures of Augie March* freed Bellow to write in a distinctively Jewish voice, but Roth was the first to use the style of stand-up comedy for a high-brow U.S. novel. Interviewed by George Plimpton at the height of the controversy around this book, Roth skirted questions about its content in an attempt to emphasize its formal, literary qualities. He described his attraction to "prose that has the turns, vibrations, intonations, and cadences, the spontaneity and ease, of spoken language, at the same time that it is solidly grounded on the page, weighted with the irony, precision, and ambiguity associated with a more traditional rhetoric."

> The conception is really nothing, you know, beside the delivery. My point is that until my "ideas"—about sex, guilt, childhood, about Jewish men and their Gentile women—were absorbed by an overall fictional strategy and goal, they were ideas not unlike anybody else's. Everybody has "ideas" for novels; the subway is jammed with people hanging from the straps, their heads full of ideas for novels they cannot begin to *write*. I am often one of them.[19]

One may take Roth at his word, since this, his third novel, was the first in a comic mode, and his later ideas for comic novels could result in very poor ones (*The Breast* and *Our Gang*). Unquestionably, it was the "delivery" of *Portnoy's Complaint* that drew attention to its targets, first among them the Freudian legacy of psychoanalysis, a therapeutic process that overcame repression through speech and was now obliged to put the genie (repression *and* speech) back into the bottle. Cast as Alexander Portnoy's presumably private revelations to his analyst, the monologues that comprise this novel are violated through public disclosure, playing on every patient's suspicion that the whole exercise is just a way of titillating the doctor and prolonging dependency. In literary terms, the "plot"—a series of sexual exploits with obsessively pursued and conquered Gentile women—traces the development of a Jewish boy from Newark, New Jersey, into a lonely thirty-three-year-old adolescent. In comic terms, it sends up the device that it exploits: "[Since] my return from Europe I have been putting myself to sleep each night in the solitary confinement of my womanless bed with a volume of Freud in my hand. Sometimes Freud in hand, sometimes Alex in hand, frequently both."[20]

Freud is the prism through which Roth spoofs the Jewish mother—another great foil of American Jewish postwar comedy. The narrator sets himself up as an archetype of what Freud called the oedipal complex, consisting of being in love with one and hating the other part of the parental pair, and describes how his mother showered him with the kind of affection she ought to have reserved for her mate. (Allen's take on this subject: "I hear that their women don't sleep with their husbands after marriage.")[21] So affected is the boy by his mother's seductive power over him that when he tries to prove his manhood in the Land of Israel, he is physically overpowered by a woman who reminds him of pictures of his mother as a young girl. "Doctor, maybe other patients dream—with me, *everything happens*. I have a life *without* latent content. The dream thing *happens*! Doctor: *I couldn't get it up in the State of Israel!* How's that for symbolism, *bubi*?"[22] Suffocating mother love does not prevent Alex from acting out his sexual fantasies with Gentile women or vividly describing their consummation, merely from assuming the responsibilities of Jewish manhood.

As opposed to the scruffy image of the Jew in comedy of the immigrant years, Roth represents Jews as the embodiments of bourgeois respectability. Dutiful fathers play neighborhood baseball on weekends; mothers keep peaches afloat in recipe-perfect Jello. Portnoy attributes his training in the discontents of civilization to the laws of kashruth: "What else, I ask you, were all those prohibitive dietary rules and regulations all about to begin with, what else but to give us little Jewish children practice in being repressed?"[23] Emblem of a U.S.-born generation that discovers the enlarged opportunities of personal freedom, Portnoy refuses to assume the parental burden.

A contemporary joke went like this. "I had dinner with my father last night, and I made a Freudian slip. I meant to say, 'Please pass the salt,' but it came out, 'You putz, you ruined my childhood.'" Another one went like this: "My parents gave me so much guilt when I was a kid. They had a bumper sticker on their car that said, 'If my son worked just a little harder, I, too, would have an honor-roll student at Jefferson High School.'"[24] Roth drew on humor in a similar vein. In the wake of *Portnoy's Complaint*, Jewish comediennes, too, announced their liberation from the role of competent wives and mothers.

True, the older generation was not inclined to laugh at Roth's comedy, and some of *Portnoy's Complaint*'s most distinguished critics were truly frightened by his send-up. "[Under] the cartoon of the Jewish joke leers the anti-Jewish stereotype," wrote the Zionist intellectual Marie Syrkin, who likened Roth's apologia for Portnoy, the predator of Gentile women, to Nazi propaganda. In Roth as in the work of Joseph Goebbels, she wrote, "the Jewish male is not drawn to a particular girl who is Gentile, but by a Gentile 'background' which he must violate sexually." No less apprehensive, Gershom Scholem, the scholar of Jewish mysticism, reviewing the book for the Hebrew daily *Haaretz*, pointed out that anti-Semites have always looked for ways of proving the degeneracy of the Jews, and here was a brash young Jew who did their work for them. Scholem, who had immigrated to Palestine from Germany in 1922, asked what price the world Jewish community was going to pay for this book.[25]

These European-generated concerns seemed widely off the mark to Roth's generation, which by 1969 was launched on a sexual revolution, women's liberation, open marriage, *Playboy* promiscuity, contraception through chemistry, gay rights, letting it all hang out, and "getting high." In many respects, therefore, *Portnoy's Complaint* may have seemed less provocation than a product of its time.

But not in all respects. In some ways, indeed, the sexual daring of *Portnoy's Complaint* was its least "offensive" quality. Just as black comedians like Richard Pryor had begun introducing profanity in acts that were more aggressive and unsettling than almost anything that had gone before—and less accommodating of "white" sensibilities—Roth through Portnoy was venturing takeoffs on Christianity that violated still-standing taboos of polite Jewish discourse. Here, for example, is Portnoy outrageously topping Allen on the subject of Gentile license and "manliness":

> Let *them* (if you know who I mean) gorge themselves upon anything and everything that moves, no matter how odious and abject the animal, no matter how grotesque or *shmutzig* or dumb the creature in question happens to be. Let them eat eels and frogs and pigs and crabs and lobsters; let them eat vulture, let them eat ape meat and skunk if they like—a diet of abominable creatures well befits a breed of mankind so hopelessly shallow and empty-headed as to drink, to divorce, and to fight with their fists. All they know, these imbecilic eaters of the execrable, is to swagger, to insult, to sneer, and sooner or later to hit. . . . You stupid *goyim*! Reeking of beer and empty of ammunition, home you head, a dead animal (formerly *alive*) strapped to each fender, so that all the motorists along the way can see how strong and manly you are.[26]

Portnoy breaks taboos not by bedding Gentiles but rather by insulting them. Now *this* was novel. There was nothing new in Jews making fun of other Jews—of Judaism, Zionism, the Jewish family, Jewish law, prayer, the Bible, or even God. But a Jew spoofing Christianity *in the language of Christians* was another matter. Repression in Jewish culture began with repressed aggression against the majority that determined one's degree of security and prosperity. Yiddish may have had its unflattering terms for Jesus, the convert Heine did a number on von Platen, and Bruce declared Jewish and goyish open to self-definition: "I'm Jewish. Count Basie's Jewish. Ray Charles is Jewish. Eddie Cantor's goyish." But not since Masada fell to the Romans had Jews gone up with such brio against the majority. Anti-Christian jokes had been reserved for *Jews* who passed over to Christianity and intramural consumption. In contrast, when Portnoy sees a picture of "Jesus floating up to Heaven in a pink nightgown" tacked up over the sink of Bubbles Girardi, he goes after Christianity more eagerly than after the girl he hopes will cure his virginity:

> The Jews I despise for their narrow-mindedness, their self-righteousness, the incredibly bizarre sense that these cavemen who are my parents and relatives have somehow gotten of their superiority—but when it comes to tawdriness and cheapness, to beliefs that would shame even a gorilla, you simply cannot top the *goyim*. What kind of base and brainless schmucks are these people to worship somebody who, number one, never existed, and number two, if he did, looking as he does in that picture, was without a doubt The Pansy of Palestine.[27]

About to test his manhood, Portnoy apparently first wants to prove his Jewish potency, and this he does in the only way he can: by establishing that he is not a goy.

True, there is something belatedly adolescent in all this; intellectually as well as emotionally, that is the stage of life in which Portnoy is stuck. Yet those who worried lest *Portnoy's Complaint* stir up Christian backlash against the Jews were as out of date as Syrkin and Scholem in their analogies with Nazi Germany. If Bruce's improvised distinctions between Jewish and goyish mocked the increasingly unstable identity of Jews in the United States, Portnoy's riffs on Christianity a decade later responded to America's declining confidence in itself as a Christian country. Roth was enough at home in the United States to know this. Humor hits a person when they are down, and Roth could hardly pass up the opportunity to include Christianity in America's rapidly expanding gallery of vulnerable targets.

From the perspective of this book, what interests me most about *Portnoy's Complaint* is its take on the subject of Jewish humor itself. Roth said that in writing the novel, he was influenced by Henny Youngman (Henry Junggman) along with the tradition of stand-up comedy that had boomed in the Catskills and was becoming a mainstay of U.S. television. At least on second reading, if not on first, the novel seems more warning than tribute, as Alex declares himself trapped in the Jewish joking that was supposed to be his salvation: "Doctor Spielvogel, this is my life, my only life, and I'm living it in the middle of a Jewish joke! I am the son in the Jewish joke—*Only it ain't no joke!*" And a little later:

> A Jewish man with his parents alive is half the time a helpless *infant*! Listen, come to my aid, will you—and quick! Spring me from this role I play of the mothered son in the Jewish joke! Because it's beginning to pall a little, at thirty-three! And also, it *hoits*, you know, there is *pain* involved, a little human suffering is being felt, if I may take it upon myself to say so—only that's the part [the comedian] Sam Levenson leaves *out*! Sure, they sit in the casino at the Concord, the women in their minks and the men in their phosphorescent suits, and boy do they laugh, laugh, and laugh—"Help, help, my son the doctor is drowning!"—ha

ha *ha*, ha ha *ha*, only what about the *pain*, Myron Cohen! What about the guy who is actually drowning![28]

Portnoy has expected his lie-down comedy to move him beyond the smothering taboos he thinks are keeping him weak and needy. But like Sholem Aleichem's monologues that end with the rabbi passing out or the listener trying to strangle the man seeking his advice, Roth's shtick overwhelms its subject. His bid for liberation fails. In the joke about the drowning son that he cites, the mother's incongruous boast punctures her and our anxieties at the moment he is going under. But

Jews and Catholics are among the favored targets of cartooning, which can identify them visually by their clothing. Courtesy of Andy Singer.

"Okay, who gets the kosher meal?"

Victimhood and the kosher laws figure in this version of gallows humor. Torture and the dietary laws represent contrasting methods of discipline and self-discipline. Courtesy of www.CartoonStock.com.

Portnoy draws our attention back to the drowning. In trying to manage the crises of Jewish experience, Jewish humor had reached a tipping point. *Portnoy's Complaint* warns that the cure, laughter, may be worse than the disease. A strategy for creative survival may have become a recipe for defeat.

As Roth might put it: Does Portnoy eat pussy and warn against it, too? First exploit the vulgarity, indulge the eroticism, roll out the high-spirited comedy, and then extravagantly confess to having failed? A preachy edge to the satire occasionally attests to another kind of failure:

> And instead of crying over he-who-has-turned-his-back
> on the saga of *his people*, weep for your own pathetic

> selves, why don't you, sucking and sucking on that sour grape of a religion! Jew Jew Jew Jew Jew! It is coming out of my ears already, the saga of the suffering Jews! Do me a favor, my people, and stick your suffering heritage up your suffering ass—*I happen also to be a human being*![29]

When he loses control over the comedy, the narrator sounds like an ordinary sap. The same may be said of the novel's final chapter, which consists in its entirety of Dr. Spielvogel's "punch line": "Now vee may perhaps to begin."[30] The book is reduced to less than the sum of its parts. Still, in the rollout of American Jewish comedy, Roth's book was the first to sound the warning that arises from among the best of its practitioners.

Under Hitler and Stalin

I told jokes, and everything inside me wept.

—Shimen Dzigan, *The Impact of Jewish Humor*

From its beginnings in the 1920s and with mounting force in the 1930s, Hitler's anti-Jewish propaganda powerfully affected neighboring Poland in the form of anti-Jewish pogroms, discriminatory laws, economic boycott, and prejudice from once-friendlier fellow citizens. Mass emigration—the time-tested Jewish answer to oppression—was blocked by closed borders in the lands of potential refuge. In a paradox characteristic of other modern Jewish societies under pressure, the growing sense of siege that pervaded the Jewish communities of Poland stimulated an already-booming culture. The Association of Jewish Writers and Journalists in Warsaw grew from a membership of sixty when it was founded in 1916 to over three hundred when the Germans invaded in 1939; it sent out speakers to Polish towns and cities while sustaining a network of competing newspapers, journals, and publishing houses in the capital. There was also an increased need for entertainment that would distract or temporarily release the tension, and offer consolation.

Professional comedy was part of this ferment. While American Jewish comedy was ripening among vacationers in the Catskills, its Polish counterpart developed in urban theaters that specialized in Jewish entertainment. The Yiddish theater attracted mixed audiences of Jews and liberal Gentiles when it performed serious plays and works from the international repertoire, but comic entertainers appealed to insiders looking for more intimate as well as lighter fare. The leading Jewish comedians in Poland, Dzigan and his partner Yisroel Schumacher, reached the peak of their fame in Warsaw in the years that Hitler was consolidating his control over Germany. As against the attempt of Yiddish "high" culture to overcome dialectical variance by imposing "Lithuanian" Yiddish as the standard language, this duo exploited the regional accents and homespun argot of their native Lodz for comedy's sake.

Through trial and error in the small-scale Yiddish chamber theater (*kamera teater*) where he made his start, Dzigan developed the comic persona of a traditional Jew, dressed in black caftan and hat with a distinctive red handkerchief as his emblem and prop—an intimate and familiar figure who could be trusted as he went about the business of spoofing his audience. How does an old-world character manage the novelties of modern life? In one routine, he came on stage playing with a yo-yo, whose many uses he demonstrated by strapping it to his arm in the form of tefillin, prayer phylacteries, then dangling it as a pocket watch on a golden chain. His wife, he explained, used the yo-yo instead of potatoes for her sabbath stew; his daughter had just given birth to yo-yo twins; but a brother-in-law couldn't have children because his yo-yo didn't work.

Dzigan's rapid-fire patter was a lot like Groucho's, but rather than neutering Jewishness for a general public he played up its specificities. Some of the duo's barbs were lifted from early Enlightenment satire, "translated and improved" (as the Yiddish theater claimed about its versions of Shakespeare's plays) to bring it up to date.

Politics became part of their stock-in-trade. In their description of a fatal hunting accident, Field Marshal Herman Göring is mistaken for a pig. Although it was safer to ridicule German than Polish targets, audiences laughed hardest at local ones. A popular routine brought onstage the anti-Semitic priest Stanislaw Tzeciak, whose agitation had often led to violence against Jews. Passing himself off as a scholar of the Talmud, Tzeciak had accused Jews of using their religion to dominate others—for example, by inventing the practice of ritual slaughter of animals as a means of controlling the meat industry. The instage priest spouts what the audience recognizes as absurd interpretations of the Talmud. As he walks offstage, he boasts of his Jewish brains—"What does the Talmud call it? Oh yes, *tukhes*." He points to his head while alluding to his rear end.

A riskier skit was "The Last Jew in Poland," which played out the consequences of anti-Semitic ethnic cleansing. An earlier dystopian novel by Hugo Bettauer, *The City without Jews*, had envisioned Vienna stripped of the creative tenth of its population. Similarly, in the Dzigan-Schumacher version, a *judenrein* Poland produces a stalled economy and decimated culture, thereby triggering a frantic attempt to reverse the process. The Jew who has been the slowest to join the exodus of his people finds himself besieged by citizens begging him to

Jolly Paupers (*Freylekhe kabtsonim*) was shot in Warsaw in 1937, at the height of Yiddish film production in Poland, starring the comic team of Shimen Dzigan and Yisroel Schumacher as schlemiels who discover oil (where someone has accidentally spilled a can). The scene being shot features actor Menashe Oppenheim in the eponymous role of Bar Kokhba, leader of the 132 CE Jewish rebellion against Rome. Courtesy of YIVO Archives.

stay. He is feted at a banquet with gefilte fish, cholent, and Jewish entertainment, and given a medal, which he promptly pins to his backside next to his Polish Cross of Merit. This "insult to the Polish nation" almost got the comedians arrested. Since the Polish censors sometimes closed offensive acts after the first performance, ticket sales were brisk for the duo's opening nights.

Reflecting on this high point in his life, Dzigan later asked himself, "How was it possible?"

> Were we deaf, dumb, and blind to the threatening signs of the times? I have no answer. I can only say that perhaps because we subconsciously felt that our verdict was sealed and our fate unavoidable, we consciously wished to shout it down and drown it out. With effervescent joy we wanted to drive off the gnawing sadness, the dread and fear that nested deep inside us.[1]

To describe this attempt to drown out their woes, Dzigan employs the term *fartumlen*, just as Americans used tummler to describe their Borscht Belt shtick.

■ Dzigan's reflections on the uses of comedy in a time of acutest danger became even more pertinent once the Hitler-Stalin pact of 1939 brought on the German invasion from the west and the Soviet onslaught from the east. Uniting the staunchest of ideological antagonists, the pact was more preposterous than anything a comedian could have invented. Jews, whose modern culture had specialized in accommodation and self-mockery, were the least equipped to imagine the pathological criminality of the Final Solution, even after they were trapped in ghettos and forced to sew yellow stars on their clothing, even after a few stragglers escaped to tell the tale from the burial pits where they and thousands of their fellow Jews had been rounded up and shot. Nor could those who had looked to socialism as the perfection of humankind believe the accounts of tyranny and terror emanating from the Soviet Union. If cognitive dissonance is caused by a divergence between convictions and actuality, and if humor attempts to exploit that discomfort, no one was ever so perfectly placed to joke as were Jews under Hitler and Stalin.

During the late 1930s and early years of the Second World War, the common repressive measures of Nazi Germany and Stalinist Russia generated much interchangeable humor. In the German version a child is asked, "What would you like to be if Hitler were your father?" "An orphan!" comes the answer—and the answer is the same when the imagined parent is Stalin.

> Two Jews, waiting before the firing squad, are informed that they are to be hanged instead. "You see," says one, "they've run out of ammunition!"[2]

> Two acquaintances meet on the street. "It's good to see you back," says the first.
>
> "I hear that conditions in the concentration camp are horrible." "Not at all," replies the second. "They wake us at 7:30. Breakfast with choice of coffee or cocoa is followed by sports or free time for reading. Then a plentiful lunch, rest period, games, a stroll, and conversation until dinner, the main meal of the day. This is followed by entertainment, usually a movie . . ."
>
> The first man is incredulous. "Really! The lies they spread about the place! I recently ran into Klein, who told me horror stories."
>
> "That's why he's back there," nods the second.

We do not know whether such jokes moved from east to west or vice versa, but they are found in both languages. The play between "getting" a joke and getting sent to a concentration camp for getting a joke dates from either the establishment of the Nazi concentration camp at Dachau in 1933 or the earlier Soviet labor camps that came to be known as the gulag. The joke, whose technique is dissimulation, exposes the need for dissimulation in order to stay alive. To the extent that humor reveals what must otherwise remain concealed, a repressive regime can be its natural incubator.

■ The German Sphere

Though Jewish humor in the late 1930s crossed otherwise-sealed frontiers, it responded differently to the two regimes. Nazism was unlike Soviet Communism in offering no enticements to Jews. Since it aimed at their elimination and held no promise of a better world for all, it attracted no Leon Trotskys to its cause. The increasing threat to Jews under German rule brought greater moral clarity. Jews were targeted as Jews, humiliated as Jews, denounced as Jews, and finally forced into Jewish ghettos and murdered as Jews. Under Nazism, therefore, Jewish humor went mainstream only among a small liberal constituency and only until the war. In the ghettos and concentration camps, under German rule, Jewish humor became more internal, hermetic, contorted, and intense than what had once circulated outside their walls.

In 1985 I joined a study trip through Poland with professors of the Hebrew University, several of whom had fled the country before the Second World War. One day, on a street in the town of Kaziemerz, as they were talking in Hebrew among themselves, they overheard one Pole remark to another, "That's how they used to speak before the war." One of the Israelis corrected him, "Not exactly. Before the war, 'we' spoke Yiddish, and now we were speaking Hebrew." The Pole replied, "But that's how you used to speak when you didn't want us to understand." This perceptive witness was accurately describing what the linguist Max Weinreich calls the linguistic style of *yehudi beloy* (Jew, beware), a way of speaking Yiddish that incorporates as many Hebrew loanwords as possible so that Gentiles who understand some Yiddish or German will be left in the dark. As Weinreich puts it (with the Hebrew in italics), "*Zay* shomea *vos der* orl *iz* magid [listen to what the Gentile is saying]" had less of a chance of being understood than the synonymous "*her vos der* goy *zogt!*"[3]

Germans and Jews both developed furtive languages—the same strategy of secretive speech being put to opposite uses by predators and intended victims, respectively. Whereas Nazism specialized in what George Orwell called doublespeak to conceal its murderous intentions, Jews under Nazi rule used *yehudi beloy* to clarify their situation. Jews developed code words to warn of approaching Germans or their henchmen, to express the horrors of death and dying, starvation and deportation. A signal that a moment of danger had passed was *nirtzeh*, the heading of that part of the Passover seder when the major part of it is over; the festive term served a practical and psychological conspiratorial function, uniting celebrants of Passover against a new pharaoh:

A bomb explodes at a meeting of Horowitz, Moyshele, and Shtolener.

Who survives?

Mankind.

It helps to know that Horowitz was a code name for Hitler, Moyshele for Benito Mussolini, and Shtolener for Stalin, the man of steel.

In common ghetto speech, Hitler was routinely referred to as Haman, villain of the biblical Book of Esther, and on the festival of Purim, when Jews eat hamantaschen to mark the evil schemer's inglorious end, ghetto Jews looked forward to devouring Hitlertaschen.

Jewish irony darkened with Jewish fate. Jews in hiding were called *lamed-vovniks*, an acronym for the legendary thirty-six (Hebrew: *lamed-vov*) saintly men for whose sake God keeps the world alive. In folktales, these anonymous just men escape notice as a feature of their humility; in ghetto irony, they escape notice in order to save their lives.

A reliance on Aryan papers (*arishe papirn*) was mocked by the addition of the consonant "n" (*narishe papirn*, meaning "foolish papers"), as though to suggest that the subterfuge was bound to be exposed.

Maxims were adapted to local conditions. To the motto inscribed over the gate at Auschwitz, *Arbeit macht frei*, Jews added *fun lebn*: "Work liberates you—from life."[4]

Wit became drier and more compressed. Ghetto Jews quipped that they had turned religious: they fast every day as on Yom Kippur, they sleep in makeshift quarters as on Sukkoth, they are riddled like matzo on Passover, and so forth. Cleverness scored the victories that the victims could not. Habits of self-deprecation persisted, but under ghetto conditions it was sometimes hard to distinguish between condemnation and reassurance. Four things are unconquerable: the German army, the British fleet, the American dollar, and Jewish smuggling. Though the fourth of these symbols of power obviously subverts our expectations, Jewish smuggling in the ghetto *was* a form of triumph over those who allowed no traffic in or out.

■ We owe our knowledge of ghetto humor to contemporary diarists and chroniclers—among others, the historian Emanuel Ringelblum and the team he assembled to preserve a record of Jewish life within the confines of the Warsaw Ghetto. Some of the joking recorded by Ringelblum was hermetic in the extreme, as in the wit of the candle seller who used the peculiarities of local pronunciation—in which *lakht* could mean either "light" or "laugh"—to advertise his wares:

> "*Lakht*, Jews, *lakht* for 20 groschen. They burn day and night without mercy. *Lakht*, Jews, *lakht* . . ." While a smiling crowd gathers in the narrow lane, the peddler shouts louder: "Buy, Jews, and may they burn on memorial days and during festive occasions, on days commemorating the dead, and God be willing, on days to commemorate the scoundrels! *Lakht*, Jews, *lakht* for 20 groschen and may Jews at long last be able to celebrate!"[5]

The dialect makes it impossible to know whether the seller is asking to be rewarded for his humor or actually expected Jews to buy candles for the named purposes. Analogously, the hallowed nature of Ringelblum's archival project, euphemistically called *Oyneg Shabes*—"celebration of the sabbath"—makes us reluctant to pluck comic items out of what was designed to be a comprehensive documentation of Jewish society and all that transpired within it. Some have even questioned the moral valence of discussing humor during the *hurbn* (Holocaust). But their worry is pointless: the Jews whose catastrophe it was could no sooner have dulled their wit than altered the fundamental powerlessness of their condition.

Vilna, for example, resembled Warsaw in boasting an extraordinarily rich prewar repertoire of folk humor, some of it playing on the several languages Jews spoke in tandem. The Vilna proverb "Three things come too late: wisdom, regret, and the fire brigade" was funnier in Yiddish, where the first two terms, *der sekhel* and *kharote*, were borrowed from Hebrew, and the final, deflationary one, *di pozharne komande*, from Polish. Similarly, by a mere flick of consonants, Vilna Jews turned a call for progress, *di tsaytn baytn zikh*—the cliché "the times they are a-changing"—into its riposte, *di baytn tsaytn zikh*—"innovations grow stale." No surprise, then, that along with songs and sayings, the Vilna Ghetto should have produced comedy revues like *Di yogenish in fas*, punning on "Diogenes [here, in two words, 'the hustle'] in a barrel." The title yoked the legendary Greek thinker, who was said to have lived in a barrel, to the reality of ghetto Jews chasing around frantically in their cramped space.

Having forged their humor to express the paradox of a chosen people repeatedly devastated by history, Jews could hardly give up their trademark invention in the hour of their greatest need. To be sure, I have no record of either a Jew facing the gallows who actually indulged in gallows humor or any Jews joking while they undressed beside the pit in which they would be shot. Humor was never the main strategy of Jewish survival, but only a chronic habit of mind. When rumors began circulating in late 1942 about the uses that Germans were making of the human fat of their victims, people said to one another, "Here's hoping we meet up on the same shelf," or "Don't worry so much about not eating. So the Germans will have a little less soap!"

Some ghetto humor acknowledged that it was playing a zero-sum game. The ghetto saying "Jews, how fortunate you are that you don't know how unfortunate you are!" congratulates Jews for the ignorance that will help to destroy them. Recorded as ghetto folklore in the Ringelblum archives of the Warsaw Ghetto is the sentiment I've quoted earlier, *Opgehit zol men vern, di milkhome zol azoy lang doyern, vi lang yidn kenen oys'haltn*, "God forbid that the war should last as long as Jews are able to endure it." To the ghetto wit who coined the joke, the vaunted Jewish capacity for survival can only be proved by constant testing, making Jewish resiliency both a response to hardship and its reinforcement. I take this expression as an acme of Jewish humor and recognition of its fatal potential. The merciless irony acknowledges that Jews had long since exceeded the bounds of normal existence.

The historian Samuel Kassow notes that the vigorous wit of the early days of the Warsaw Ghetto became more and more attenuated toward the end.[6] Avrom Karpinovitch, who assisted Dzigan in writing his autobiography, recalls the first appearance of Dzigan and Schumacher on their return to Lodz in 1947, two years after the end of the war. In the performance hall were remnants of the almost quarter-million Jews who once constituted this second-largest Jewish community in Europe. When the duo entered from opposite sides of the stage, Dzigan opened with the usual, *Abi men zet zikh!*, "As long as we meet again!" but instead of the usual laughter in response, the audience wept. On that occasion it took some time before the humor took hold.

■ The Soviet Sphere

When Poland was attacked simultaneously by the Nazis and Communists, Dzigan and Schumacher were among the relatively fortunate Jews who fled to the Soviet sphere. Since they could no longer perform in bombed and besieged Warsaw, they made their way to Kharkov and then Moscow, where they were welcomed and for a short time allowed to perform. Trained to recognize and exploit discrepancies between propaganda and reality, they were surprised to discover that so great was that gap in the so-called Worker's Paradise, Soviet Jewish folk humor was way ahead of them.

> "What is the difference between Kolkhoz, the collective farm, and Kol Nidrei, the Yom Kippur prayer?"
>
> "Kol Nidrei means you don't eat for a day; Kolkhoz means you don't eat for a year."

Another witticism had it that there were three categories of citizen: those who sit, those who sat, and those who have yet to sit, the Yiddish *zitsn* meaning to sit in prison. In still another, Russia was likened to a streetcar where some can sit while the rest stand shaking. Even as they picked up these nuggets, the comedians were warned against ever indulging in such comedy, not only on stage, but also even among trusted friends. When Dzigan once privately joked about local conditions to the noted Yiddish poet Peretz Markish, he was scolded, "When you escaped the Germans you saved your skin. Now you must save your life."[7]

Jewish experience was never as contorted as under Soviet rule. All universalizing ideologies, whether regressive or progressive, oppose Judaism for its refusal to comply with their transcendent or homogenizing plans, but the Communist International expected Jews, because they had "no country of their own," to lead the way in dissolving their collective identity. Communists with a Jewish past, like Karl Marx and Trotsky, were often the most extreme in forcing compliance on their own kind. The practice of religion was prohibited for all Soviet citizens, but Jews were forbidden, in addition to synagogue attendance and prayer, such religious-national markers as circumcision, kosher and Passover diet, observance of sabbath and the Jewish calendar, the use of Hebrew, and Talmudic study. As elsewhere in the world the modern Zionist drive for Jewish national self-liberation gathered strength, Stalin established a "Jewish autonomous region" that was supposed to provide an alternative Jewish homeland on the Manchurian border. Meanwhile, anti-Semitism, officially outlawed, persisted among the leadership and public at large.

The contradictions of Communist life may well have been experienced by Jews more acutely than by other Soviet citizens, all of whom were instructed to adjust to a new concept of humankind. When Marx identified capitalism with the Jews, he was inadvertently acknowledging the strengths of Jews and capitalism alike. The Jewish way of life did indeed encourage many of the same features that exemplify capitalist society, described by one scholar as "innovativeness, willingness to take risk, and willingness to defer gratification through savings and education."[8] To these might be added another characteristic: gratification though humor. If Jews enjoyed a certain advantage in adapting to liberal democracies with their free market economies and incentives for initiative, the same features of Jewish life also helped them adapt to Soviet rule—except that adaptation in this case required *undoing* the way of life that had given Jews their skills of adaptation in the first place. Humor battened on contradictions like the one attributed to Moscow's Rabbi Jacob Mazeh, playing on the Bolshevik leader's change of his family name: "The Trotskys make the Revolution; the Bronsteins pay the bill." The new totalistic faith would prove disastrous to Judaism, just as previous such challenges had done.

Yiddish, the Jewish vernacular, created further complications. As I have already noted, Yiddish became differentiated from German and other European languages to the degree that Jews followed a way of life distinct from that of their Gentile neighbors. The separate language then reinforced the separateness that brought it into being. Yet Soviet rulers declared Yiddish the national language of the Jews at the expense of Hebrew so that it could serve as the vehicle of Sovietization and help to *expunge* their Jewishness. While this predicament applied to all Russia's ethnic minorities—whose languages remained irreducible proof of the separate identities they were being asked to abjure—Yiddish was simultaneously the language of Jews throughout the world, many of whom retained close ties to Russia and Russian Jewish culture. For a time the Communist International used this Jewish international language to spread its message, providing Yiddish with government support that gave Soviet Yiddish writers an advantage over Yiddish writers in non-Communist Poland and the Americas. Several important Yiddish writers returned to Russia on that account. But the apple was poisoned: once the regime had more to hide than to advertise, the Yiddish writers were denounced as counterrevolutionaries on account of the foreign contacts they had been encouraged to establish. Soviet advantage worked the way that Yiddish enhances blessings as a prelude to aggravating the curse: "May you have the juiciest goose, but no teeth; the best wine, but no sense of taste; and the most beautiful wife, but be impotent."[9]

In one respect, however, Communism did accomplish its egalitarian and integrationist aims. The common experience of Sovietization turned Jewish humor into a popular Russian genre, and certain anthropological affinities between Jews and Slavs made for an easier interpenetration of their humor than was ever possible between Yiddish and German. The Jewish *glaykhvort* morphed into the Russian *anekdot*: "A Muscovite boasts of having been hired as a lookout in one of the Kremlin towers, keeping watch for the dawn of the world revolution. Asked if he isn't bored in that occupation, he replies: 'Yes, but it's the ultimate in job security.'" This is adapted from a Yiddish joke about the shtetl Jew who is hired for a few kopeks a day to keep watch for the messiah. Asked about the paltry salary, he replies, "Yes, but it's permanent work." The crack has been attributed to the Hebrew poet Micah Joseph Lebensohn (1828–52), when as a young prodigy, he was jokingly offered this same job by the Vilna scholar Matthew Strashun.[10] The joke crossed cultural boundaries with no apparent self-consciousness; in each case, the promise of eternal security undermines the system's redemptive claims.

To judge from their prominence in its creation, dissemination, and interpretation, the percentage of Jews in the making of Russian humor may have approached U.S. levels. Odessa was considered its capital:

> "How many Jews are there in Odessa?"
> "Five-hundred thousand."
> "And the rest of the population?"
> "Jewesses."

> "What's the population of Odessa?"
> "One-and-a-half million."
> "How many Jews?"
> "What are you, deaf?"[11]

The overrepresentation of Jews in Russian comedy became so embarrassing that at a national gathering of Soviet humorists,

Jewish delegates were urged to make jokes about other nationalities. One of them began to improvise, "Two Chinese are walking along the shores of the Yangtse River and one says to the other, "Listen, Haim . . ."

Joking aside, however, Soviet rulers may have initially permitted humor as an escape valve—a common explanation for the toleration of comedy in dictatorial regimes—but by 1927 they had imposed laws making satire punishable by imprisonment or worse. Joking in Russia became much more dangerous than drinking in the United States during Prohibition. Nadezhda Mandelstam, widow of the doomed poet Osip Mandelstam, recalled the first time that the couple heard the expression "Give us a man, and we'll make a case." It was in 1928 at a health resort, where two of their fellow guests were playing at Interrogation, a game of their own invention.[12] One of the men had served in the "exterminating profession" (the CHEKA); the other was a so-called Nepman who had taken advantage of Vladimir Ilyich Lenin's New Economic Policy to engage in petty trade, only to be arrested, as so many were, once the policy was repudiated. Reconstructing the roles they had performed in real life, the two men derive quite a thrill from their playacting.

Mandelstam's own 1933 parodic poem on Stalin, the barely disguised "Kremlin mountaineer," elicited a similar thrill when he shared it with a circle of friends. Oral forms of humor were somewhat protected by anonymity and their ephemeral nature, but the literary species enjoyed no such protection. Some satirists, like Ilya Ehrenburg (*The Stormy Life of Lasik Roitschwantz*, 1927) and Ilya Ilf and Evgeny Petrov

(*The Twelve Chairs*, 1928), managed to escape retribution. But most, including Mandelstam, did not. He was exiled twice, and the second time, in 1938, he succumbed to the intended consequence.

■ Phases of Russian Jewish Humor

Soviet Jewish humor evolved over its seven decades in response to political changes. The first phase was the brightest, despite the catastrophic ruin that had overtaken so many Jewish communities during the First World War, the Russian civil war, and the Russian-Polish war of 1919–20. In the immediate aftermath of the Bolshevik revolution, many young Jews were more captivated by the innovative spirit of the times than troubled by the toll it was taking on their coreligionists.

Already on the eve of the revolution, the writer Babel, mentioned briefly in the introduction and discussed more later in this chapter, had predicted that Russian literature's messiah, so long awaited, would emerge from Odessa's "sun-drenched steppes washed by the sea." He was referring to himself, a native son of that Jewish city. Babel's writings uncovered a jovial form of Jewishness everywhere he looked—in the overcrowded, impoverished ghetto, among the "fat and funny bourgeois lying in the evening on couches in front of their funny, philistine dachas," amid the *luftmenschen* roaming the coffeehouses and the company of the underworld toughs of the Moldavanka. Babel drew inspiration from Hershele Ostropolier, playing the Jewish rogue so successfully that he excited the ire of the cavalry hero General Semyon Budyonny and Stalin himself. Literary mischief couldn't get much riskier than that.

Marc Chagall emerged from a similar amalgam of Russian Jewishness, bringing a brightening burst of color to his birthplace, Vitebsk. In the marvelous way that art conducts its own conversation across time and space, Chagall's piebald fiddler was later adopted as the iconic image of *Fiddler on the Roof*—as noted earlier, a musical inspired by Sholem Aleichem, whose works had been adapted by the Moscow Art Theater with sets designed by Chagall. Very much in Sholem Aleichem's spirit, Chagall's story was all about beating the odds, beginning with the traditional Jewish boy who becomes a modern artist and proceeds merrily to turn the world upside down. In Chagall's art, levitating bridegrooms have their heads turned around as in the Yiddish expression *zi hot im fardreyt dem kop*, though Chagall knew that the Yiddish phrase meant not "she turned his head" but rather "she drove him crazy." In Chagall's cemeteries, as in Sholem Aleichem's, you can hear the intimate exchanges among those who lie beneath gravestones that tilt like inclining ears. And Chagall was only one of several Russian Jewish artists who developed a genre of visual wit in book design, illustration, and art.[13]

That was all at the beginning. A second, darker phase of Jewish humor developed once Stalin replaced Lenin, and started enforcing collectivization and compliance:

> After Stalin's takeover of Soviet leadership, the Politburo receives a repentant telegram from Trotsky. Kalinin [of

> Russian peasant stock] reads it aloud. "I made mistakes and you didn't. You were right and I was wrong." Members are about to applaud when up jumps Kaganovich [one of Stalin's chief supporters in the struggle against Trotsky]: "You've misread the telegram. It reads: *I* made mistakes and you *didn't*? *You* were right and I was *wrong*?"[14]

Yiddish has several comic versions of such "corrected" telegrams, which lacking punctuation, depend for their interpretation on the intonation of the reader. These jokes draw attention to the mechanism that substitutes an unexpected (ironic) construal for the obvious (declarative) one. That Kaganovich and Trotsky are both Jews hints at the cultural intimacy that sets them apart from Soviet Gentiles, despite their fealty to the Communist International; Kaganovich's vindictiveness in exposing his fellow Jew; and the fear of implication that may have prompted his preemptive malice against his coreligionist. The motif of misreading underscores the importance of deciphering the politburo's official utterances.

Russians also joked about features of czarism that persisted in Soviet guise. In that vein, Jews mocked the persistence of aggression aimed specifically at them.

> What is "friendship among Soviet nationalities?"
>
> Armenians join with Russians, Russians with Ukrainians, and Ukrainians with Uzbeks to beat up the Jews.

Or more subtly: "Haim is walking down the street when someone calls him a Jew bastard. He mutters: 'Ay, if only there were meat in the shops, it would be like czarist times.'"

The faux nostalgia embeds this joke about the persistence of anti-Semitism in the gibe that czarism was better than its replacement.

As for what may be considered *anti*-Jewish humor, Jews themselves served up most, if not all, of it for their own bitter amusement, and it was probably most appreciated by them. This may have been particularly the case with Jewish commissars who were sufficiently self-conscious and nervous about their overrepresentation in high party positions to spoof their own telltale accents and prominence, and with intellectuals who indulged in irony as a habit of mind.

The boundaries between laughing at and laughing with became increasingly permeable in Soviet humor, just as happened in the United States but under contrasting circumstances. The Communist system controlled the movement of Soviet subjects, invaded private life, and mistrusted the instincts of the populace. As prohibitions forced open dissent into subversive channels, Jewish-style political humor became something of a national pastime:

> What is a Soviet optimist?
> Someone without all the facts.[15]

Jokes about Abram, Chaimovitch, or Rabinovitch became widespread. Acquired habits of quiescence, a familiar foil of Jewish comedy, became rampant in a punitive regime:

> Passing KGB headquarters, Abram sighs.
> "Abram," whispers his wife, "how many times have I told you not to make political pronouncements in public."

The wily generic Jew trying to outsmart the authorities was now a model for every Soviet citizen:

> As soon as Abram arrives in Moscow, he cables his wife at home in Berdichev: DON'T REVEAL LOCATION OF BURIED BOX IN YARD. Several hours later his frantic wife calls to tell him that KGB agents are digging up their backyard. "Don't worry, my dear," Abram calms her. "I only wanted to make spring planting easier for you."

> At the ostentatious funeral of a high Communist official that is reputed to have cost the state about 100,000 rubles, a Jew says indignantly, "What about the policy of economizing? For that price, I could bury the whole Central Committee."[16]

Studies of the Russian anekdot during this period highlight its resistance to the "existential totalism to which state ideology aspired."[17] Jewish humor had specialized in this kind of resistance under earlier punitive systems, and with the greatly increased social interaction between Jews and other Russians, Jewish jokes naturally leached into the public domain, even as some Slavic humor was absorbed in Jewish humor.

We are told that Stalin himself enjoyed jokes, like the one about a delegation from his native Georgia that conducts an interview with him and then takes its leave. Stalin starts looking for his pipe and can't find it. He calls in Lavrenty Pavlovich Beria, the dreaded head of his secret police, and instructs him to go after the delegation and uncover the thief. Beria rushes off down the corridor. Five minutes later Stalin finds his pipe under a pile of papers. He calls Beria—"Look, I've found my pipe." "It's too late," Beria says, "half the delegation admitted they took your pipe, and the other half died during questioning."

A third phase of Soviet Jewish humor was ushered in by Israel's defeat of the Soviet-backed Arabs in 1967. Jews who had traditionally cast themselves as comic foils now emerged as the improbable "victors" in a society increasingly frustrated by its authorities' incompetence and repression.

> The instructor in the Russian War College was discussing how the Soviet Union might win a war against China. Perplexed, a student asked how their military could stack up against China's inexhaustible manpower. "It is possible for the smaller army to win," the instructor said, citing the example of the recent Six-Day War: "Israel can field a maximum of two or three million against the Arabs' hundred million and yet it won that war."
>
> "Yes," the student objected, "but where can we find three million Jews?"[18]

The Russians telling this joke (or the Jews imagining their fellow Russians telling this joke) were mocking themselves in the way that Jews had traditionally made fun of their own weaknesses, suggesting that for the first time, Jews may have gained a *political* advantage over their Gentile compatriots. The irony of this newfound Jewish advantage quickened once the movement for emigration to Israel gave the Jews a destination of freedom, and Russians hoping to be included in the exodus began to advertise for Jewish grandmothers: "A group of resourceful Georgians forge Soviet internal passports intending to apply for exit visas to Israel. They are discovered. As punishment, they have to keep their Jewish nationality."[19]

Kulbak and Babel

The contortions of doublespeak that were required for everyday survival in the Soviet Union produced some comic masterworks by writers willing to risk (or unable to avoid risking) their lives. The contortions may have been played out to their fullest in the work and career of the Yiddish poet and writer Kulbak, whose comic novel *Zelmenyaners* I introduced briefly in chapter 2.

Kulbak's talent benefited and suffered from some of the choices that he made in the tumultuous 1920s. Educated in both a Russian Jewish school and yeshiva, Kulbak, a bookish young man attracted to nature, took full advantage of the revolutionary moment to experiment with various literary genres as well as styles of poetry and prose, the most successful of which played off the tensions between his lyric sensibility and skeptical intelligence. He was among the many eastern European writers and artists who spent time in Berlin in the postwar years 1918–21, soaking up its expatriate atmosphere and trying his hand at Yiddish expressionism. He then moved back to his native region, where he taught literature in the Jewish Teachers' Seminary, winning the love of Vilna's Jewish youths and all the while publishing works that ran the gamut from radical modernism to modern balladry. When

Kulbak decided to cross from Polish Vilna to Soviet Minsk in 1928, perhaps to join some of his family, he may also have hoped to gain publishing opportunities in the only place where Yiddish writers and scholars received government support. Had he not moved to the Soviet Union, he could not have written *Zelmenyaners*, the masterwork that sealed his doom.

Zelmenyaners divides its affections and barbs between the twin phenomena of declining Jewishness and the hardening rule of Stalin's Soviet state. The family of Reb Zelmele (diminutive of Zalman) hails, as did Kulbak himelf, from the agricultural heartland of Belarus, where over time its members had developed their own smell—"a faint odor of musty hay mixed with something else."[20] Now they have become city folk, inhabiting a courtyard called the *REBZEHOYF* (Zelemele's *hoyf*, or yard, an imitation of Soviet speak that formed acronyms for everything). The novel's faux-anthropological description of the clan conjures up a biologically distinctive people and its adaptation to the new Soviet regimen—an adaptation that is more like a struggle against the force of historical inevitability.

As against Sholem Aleichem's famous cycle of Tevye stories, which is organized around daughters, Kulbak's revolves around Zelmele's grown sons, four "uncles" who work at tailoring, watchmaking, carpentry, and tanning, and their children, who serve in the militia, study engineering, marry Gentiles, and join the Communist Party. There is but one holdout in the younger generation: Tsalel, diminutive of Bezalel. The biblical figure Bezalel was the artist-builder of the tabernacle in the desert; Tsalel, in contrast, is a self-parody of the Soviet Yiddish writer, "too educated to do anything but read, the kind of modern young pedant who's always asking you to repeat what you've said so that he can write it down in a notebook . . . and [who] had the habit of occasionally committing suicide—which is, however, another story."[21]

Kulbak's plot turns on conflicts over tradition and innovation in the two generations. While the dictates of the state guarantee the dreary outcome of every such conflict, the storyteller lingers on the vagaries of compliance—as, for example, with the advent of electricity:

> Uncle Itshe stepped outside, glanced around to see if anyone was looking, and headed for the quiet space between Uncle Yuda's and the stable. Once it had been pitch-black. Now it was bright as day, making Itshe realize that a sanitary convenience had been lost forever. Angrily he turned back toward the yard, disgruntled by the new-fangled world.[22]

The narrator records as funny what the older generation experiences as tragic, and twits them for thinking that it is.

But the young also come in for their share of mockery. Itshe's son Bereh, a Paul Bunyan type, refuses to have his son circumcised and names him Marat for the most radical of the French revolutionaries. By adding a Yiddish diminutive to his name, Bereh's mother turns the presumptive Bolshevik into little *Maratl.* The suppressed Jewish element breaks through as well in Bereh's report to his army superiors on how he got separated from his unit:

> That same night I left for Krinitsa. From Krinitsa it was a day's walk to Buchach. From Buchach I walked to Nozerovo. From Nozerovo I walked to Diatly. From Diatly I walked to Hayduchok. From Hayduchok I walked to a village named Drozdovo. From Drozdovo I walked to Bistrich. From Bistrich I walked to Ivye. From Ivye I walked to Sokolka. In Sokolka I went to see my mother's uncle, who lives on the main street and deals in horses.[23]

Echoing chapter 33 of the Book of Numbers, which tracks the Israelites as they set out from Rameses and camp at Sukkoth, set out from Sukkoth and camp at Etham, and so forth, Bereh's deposition mocks at once the forty-five mind-numbing verses of the Bible, and the degree to which the new Soviet Jew faithfully echoes his native religion even as he serves its secularized and dictatorial replacement.

In the book's longest-running joke, Tsalel the transcriber of Zelmenyaner lore (who affects a forelock like the one that Kulbak himself sported) is forever committing suicide in unrequited love for his cousin Tonke, the most doctrinaire Marxist among the younger generation. The story's exuberance dissipates by the time Tsalel finally does commit suicide at the end of book 2. Tonke, by then a rising commissar, denounces her dead cousin for having wasted his spirit trying to preserve bits and pieces of a defunct civilization, and in a scene uncomfortably true to the Soviet culture of the 1930s, excoriates the family for wasting resources by uselessly occupying its inherited space.

Three years after the publication of this book, Kulbak was himself denounced, tried, and executed.

Kulbak's humor owed much to Sholem Aleichem, but though Sholem Aleichem's Tevye the Dairyman often chases after his horse, the smell of the creature's excrement never invades the page. Tevye's companionship with a God to whom he matters helps him prevail over the loss of his daughters and offsets some of the humiliation he must endure. In contrast, the aroma of "something else" that identifies the Zelmenyaner family is Kulbak's apology for the lingering stench of Jewish tribalism in the fresh Soviet air. Every death of an elderly Zelmenyaner in the novel is accompanied by the author's conspiratorial wink. Tsalel is the only one of them whose burial elicits a hint of tenderness:

> On a fence in a narrow street near the cemetery stood a bird without a name, though Tsalel had fought all his life to have it called *shperl*. While its tedious chirp was no substitute for Chopin's funeral march, the nameless bird was sufficiently educated to declaim from the fence several well-known lines from the collected works of Heine, Vol. I, p. 457:
>
> *Keine Messe wird man singen* — No Mass will be sung
> *Keinen Kadosch wird man sagen,* — No kaddish recited,
> *Nichts gesagt und nichts gesungen* — Nothing will be said or sung
> *Wird an meinen Sterbetagen.* — On my dying.
>
> A pair of drunken Jews performed Tsalel's last rites. No one tipped the gravediggers, though they stood by their shovels looking sharply at the mourners. It simply didn't occur to anyone.[24]

It was Kulbak himself who had tried to get *shperl* accepted as the Yiddish term for "sparrow" as part of his lifelong drive to provide his native language with a complete vocabulary for the natural world. He is also here to remind us that Jewish gravediggers had once made a living from charity, said to redeem from death—a custom now redundant, like all Jewish ritual. In tipping his hat to Heine, the greatest influence on modern Yiddish verse—the scholar intruding into the elegiac description—he reminds us of something else as well. Like Heine, who left his people without being accepted by another, Kulbak, too, realized that Communism had forced Jews to pay a "conversion" fee without granting them its promised rewards.

Still, even anticipating the worst, Kulbak could not have foreseen his arrest in 1937 at the start of Stalin's purges and the ignominy of the secret trial that sentenced him to execution on October 29 of that year. The circumstances of that execution were acknowledged only after the fall of the Soviet Union, many decades later, but meanwhile the novelist had written his obituary in his comic portrayal of the fate of a Jewish poet under Communism.

■ Only once in my adult life was I reduced to such laughter that I had to put down the book. It was a collection of short stories by the Russian Jewish writer Babel. The tale was "Di Grasso" (1937), one of Babel's many "initiation stories." Though I quote its opening paragraph here in a clearer translation than the one I read, more than usual attention is required to get the gist:

> I was fourteen years old. I belonged to the fearless battalion of theater ticket scalpers. My boss was a shark with an eye that always squinted and a large, silky mustache. His name was Kolya Shvarts. I fell in with him that dark year when the Italian Opera in Odessa went bust. The impresario, swayed by the theater critics, had not signed up Anselmi and Tito Ruffo as guest stars, concentrating instead on a strong ensemble. He was punished for this, went broke, and so did we [scalpers]. To set things right, we were promised Chaliapin, but Chaliapin wanted three thousand a performance. So Di Grasso, the Sicilian tragic actor, came with his troupe instead. They were taken to their hotel in carts loaded with children, cats, and cages in which Italian birds fluttered.
>
> "We can't push this merchandise!" Kolya Shvarts said when he saw the motley procession rolling in.[25]

The narrator, speaking autobiographically as "Isaac Babel," recalls a time about 1910 when he, a Jewish boy from a respectable family, stood at the perilous intersection of art and commerce—scalping tickets for opera and melodrama. At the center of the action is the performance of a Sicilian melodrama starring Di Grasso himself in the role of a village shepherd whose true love betrays him with Giovanni, the proverbial handsome man from town. Only about fifty people have shown up at the premiere, and until this point, the performance has been a dud. But then:

> In the third act, Giovanni, the visitor from town, met his fate. The village barber was shaving Giovanni as he sat

> with his powerful masculine legs sprawled out over the proscenium. The pleats of his vest shone beneath the Sicilian sun. The stage set portrayed a village fair. The shepherd stood in the far corner. He stood there silently, among the carefree crowd. He hung his head, then raised it, and under the weight of his burning, fixed gaze, Giovanni began to fidget and squirm in his chair. He jumped up and pushed the barber away. In a cracking voice Giovanni demanded that the policeman remove all shady and suspicious-looking people from the village square. The shepherd—played by Di Grasso—hesitated for a moment, then smiled, soared into the air, flew over the stage of the Odessa City Theater, alighted on Giovanni's shoulders, and sunk his teeth into his neck. Muttering and squinting at the audience, he sucked the blood from the wound.[26]

It was at this spot in my reading that my muscles gave way. That malevolent smile and catapult across the stage was funnier than anything I had expected. Behind the actor's lunge was the author's glee: he had drawn the bow and fired the shot that sank the poor villain, setting off the helpless reader. The irrepressible joy of that revenge was like the improbable reversal of superior jokes. In fact, at that point the whole story turns a corner. The troupe's next performances are sold out. The boy's precarious situation is resolved: he had lifted his father's watch and pawned it with his unreliable boss, Shvarts (Black), who will not return it until Shvarts's wife persuades him to do so. Relations between this Shvarts and this wife, "a woman as robust as a grenadier and as drawn out as a steppe, with a crinkled, sleepy face peeking out at its borderland," are as mysteriously passionate as those played out on the theater stage. This laughter-inducing art compresses the swoon of melodrama into the vise of wit and makes us feel, like the boy, that we are seeing life for the first time "as it really was."[27]

Of course, had the audience laughed *in the story*, the performance would have bombed. Babel's artistic catapult corresponds to Di Grasso's leap but reverses the mood, so that a mortal injury onstage has a hilarious effect on those reading about it. The narrator is working at emotional cross-purposes to the subject, much in the same way that the cartoon mouse Jerry invites laughter when he wounds Tom the cat. Humor, a permissible form of aggression, can work at the expense of those being pummeled.

But there is more to it than that. In "Di Grasso" the author's relation to *his* enterprise and readership complicates the relation between the narrator and his subject. Babel the writer professes to be offering the same kind of merchandise as the scalpers—namely, salvaged seconds from Europe's finery that seem better suited to the flea market than to the Temple of Art. The dramatic tension of the story derives from a high-stakes gamble: that great art can beat all odds. The comedy exposes how much is at risk where you least expect it.

How much was at risk? At the time of writing, Babel was in danger of losing not his shirt in the way of the scalpers in the "dark year" of the story but rather his life in the Soviet Union purges that Stalin was then swinging into high gear.

Beginning in 1928, and with increasing severity, the Communist state apparatus had been enforcing Stalin's decree that writers and artists serve its political purposes. Writers like Kulbak and Babel could hardly have anticipated the penalties for perceived deviation. In a 1934 speech at the Congress of Soviet Writers, published in *Pravda*, Babel flirted dangerously with Stalin's directives for art: "Respect for the reader. I am suffering from a hypertrophy of that feeling. I respect the reader so much that it makes me numb and I fall silent. And so I keep silence."[28] Babel's listeners laughed, yet his irony was suspect. "Anti-Soviet agitation and propaganda," with satire or mockery emphatically included under the same rubric, had been made punishable under Article 58/10 of the Soviet criminal code.[29] The man with the bushy mustache had Babel killed on January 27, 1940. I have no doubt that my knowledge of Babel's fate contributed to my tension and its release in reading the story, as though I felt, through Di Grasso's lunge, the author's joyous revenge on the man who stole away his sweet life.

■ Postwar Humor

The precarious function of humor under conditions of mortal threat is the subject of Jurek Becker's novel *Jacob the Liar*, published in Communist East Germany in 1969—the same year as *Portnoy's Complaint* in the United States. A contemporary of Roth, Becker (1937–97) was born in Poland, survived the war years in the Lodz Ghetto, and afterward remained in East Berlin, trying to earn his living as a writer in the German Democratic Republic for media that were as strictly controlled as under Stalin.

Becker's father, who had survived with him, urged his son to write a work extolling the heroism of a ghetto acquaintance who had kept a radio in defiance of Nazi decree. Becker instead produced a comic study of a man, Jacob, who *pretends* to have a concealed radio. Having once heard—during his interrogation in the German police station—a snippet of news of the advancing Red Army, Jacob uses its promise of liberation to dissuade his friend Kowalski from rushing toward certain death. Jacob is made the unwitting source of hope for a widening circle of those let in on the "secret," based on Kowalski's assumption, that he owns a radio. He keeps supplying invented news, scoring an occasional miniature victory, as when he retrieves a scrap of newspaper from a German privy. Jacob dare not disabuse the ghetto inhabitants of their faith in his lies without puncturing the hope that his lies alone can supply. Deception becomes the ghetto's lifeline much as Becker's humorous inversions keep us enjoying a story about mass murder.

In fact, Becker found in the tale of *Jacob the Liar* a means of subverting Soviet-German censorship. Camouflaging the parabolic application of the novel to repressive East German rule, he compared it instead to the Jewish condition before the war. Jacob reflects: "Had I been born more intelligent or imaginative like Sholem Aleichem—what am I saying, even half as much would have been enough—I would be able to invent ten times more and better than those who write in the newspaper."[30] This suggests that both Jacob and the author are in the tradition of the Yiddish humorist whose comic "inventions" for the readers of their day were likewise meant to obscure reality.

But was this true? Whether or not Sholem Aleichem's humor encouraged Jewish self-deception, at a time when there were still alternatives to the European constraints that were hemming the Jews in, the function of much of the joking under Hitler and Stalin was rather the opposite—to free some truth from within a punishing system of lies. In the spirit of what Germans called *flusterwitze* (whispered jokes), it expressed otherwise-forbidden feelings and knowledge.

Freud describes *galgenhumor* (gallows humor) as the ego's refusal to be compelled to suffer, to accept distressing reality. "It insists that it cannot be affected by the traumas of the external world; it shows, in fact, that such traumas are no more than occasions for it to gain pleasure."[31] This may be insightful as far as it goes, and helps to account for the pleasure of a joke like the one about two Jews before the firing squad who are asked whether they have a final wish. One asks for a cigarette. The other says, "Shush, Moshe! Don't make trouble." Turning the occasion inward to mock the excesses of Jewish passivity and accommodation momentarily obscures the executioner's threat, offering the ego the momentary pleasure of mastery over humiliation. More than supplying pleasure, joking in extremis could also speak truth where power was wielded through webs of deception and truth was forcibly prohibited.

In the end, though, whether the exercise of wit made the best of a doomed situation or encouraged fatalism depended on the real possibilities of escape. If it accommodated a threat that might otherwise have been overcome, humor was lethal; if it was truly a last resort, it could be restorative. Becker's post-Holocaust comedy evades the problem by describing an outcome that history had already determined. In his novel, Kowalski and Jacob do not escape death. To that degree, Becker's depiction of creative lying and its (limited) uses may have alerted readers in the German Democratic Republic to the direness of their own condition.

With the passage of time after the end of the war and absorption of the enormity of genocide, however, "Holocaust humor" came into its own, especially in the West. The passage of the years was bound to suppress moral inhibitions about handling this material, and reduce, if not eliminate, considerations of decency or truth. Every branch of art would sooner or later make use of the greatest massacre ever staged—and before long, political demagogues would be denying that any such mass murder had taken place, aiming not for humor but rather for intensified damage to Jews and the Jewish state. That has left it to the exercise of sound judgment to distinguish good taste from bad in fiction, film, and other genres and media.

Feel-good comedy about the murder of European Jewry is almost inevitably reductive kitsch, as in, for example, Roberto Benigni's movie *Life Is Beautiful* (1997). But what about films like Charlie Chaplin's *The Great Dictator* (1940), Ernst Lubitsch's *To Be or Not to Be* (1942), or Mel Brooks's *The Producers* (1968)? As satires of Hitler and Nazism, their appeal depends on our removal from the scene. The first two films, produced just before and during the war that the United States fought against Hitler and Nazism, were too raw for contemporary critics and audiences. They did not find it funny when the actor playing Hitler in the Lubitsch comedy says, "Heil me!" Al-

"Springtime for Hitler" number from Mel Brooks's production of *The Producers*. In the film, the audience slowly moves from horror to laughter as it realizes the show is a send-up, and this same process was reenacted in the script's reception as humor about the Holocaust became more acceptable. Courtesy MPTV images.

though Lubitsch considered this kind of humor a weapon in the war, exposing the weakness of those who claimed German invincibility, critics accused him of making fun of the tragedy.

The Producers was not originally popular at the box office, either, even though it won Brooks the Academy Award for best original screenplay. But both the film and its spin-off musical gained traction over time, just as, in the movie itself, an audience watching a performance of "Springtime for Hitler" is initially shocked by its audacity, then confused and uncertain about how to react, and finally relieved and amused to discover that they are expected to laugh. Timing matters not only *in* these films but also in relation to the events they spoof, indicating that certain satire turns funny only after time has dulled its sting. Ecclesiastes (3:4) is right about this as about so much else: there is a time to laugh, and there is a time to refrain from laughing. Blessed is the society that learns to distinguish the difference.

Hebrew Homeland

There is no subject in the world that the Jewish joke will not target.

—Danny Kerman, Israeli artist

"There is not a great deal of humor being created in Israel, and most of what exists is not very funny, at least not to non-Israelis." Joseph Telushkin's opinion is widely shared. So, too, is his explanation for the alleged dearth of Israeli wit: that Jews in Israel can deal with their problems directly and don't have to settle for the substitute gratifications of humor. "Israelis, for example, don't joke much about their Arab opponents; they fight them."[1]

This deduction is based on two interlocking assumptions: the relation of Jewish humor to powerlessness, and the relation of Israel to power. According to the first, one wouldn't joke if one could get things done. Does not Sholem Aleichem's Tevye the Dairyman rely on humor in inverse proportion to the control he wields over his life? At the loss of a daughter he fillips, "Whatever God does is for the best. That is, it had better be, because try changing it if you don't like it!"[2] Tevye mocks his failure to keep his daughters in line the way other cultures make fun of the cuckold for his inability to rule his presumptive domain. His comedy turns resignation into acquiescence.

Along the same lines, Reik, writing after the Second World War, finds in Jewish humor "not only something serious, which is present in the wit of other nations too, but sheer horror." By horror, Reik means the crushing forces that prevented Jews from determining their fate and turned them into the "marionettes of history," unable to save their children from the lime pits and crematoriums. Reik believes that only through joking are puppets transformed into human beings. "Yehovah has forbidden the Jew of our time to express his tragic experiences in a way appealing to a world that is hostile, or, at best, indifferent. But by conferring upon him the gift of wit, his God has given him the power to speak of what he suffers."[3]

By this logic, the need for Tevye's jokey acquiescence in his personal powerlessness or wit as creative compensation for political impotence would disappear once Jews gained independence in a land of their own. But this brings us to the second assumption—that Israel supplies Jewish power.

Zionism was indeed built on the hope that Jews would control their destiny once they recovered their ancestral homeland. The Zionist project was daunting, envisioning a radical break with Jewish life in the Diaspora. National liberation required of Jews not merely political consolidation, as had occurred in nineteenth-century Italy and Germany, or the reclaiming of independence, as with Polish nationalism, but rather a complete geopolitical, cultural, and psychological reversal. Moving in the millions from communities they had come to regard as home, leaving ancestral graves behind, Jews would have to drain the swamps of the Land of Israel and make its desert bloom, turn the language of their sacred texts back into their everyday vernacular, and assume responsibilities for political functions they had been delegating to others for almost two millennia.

Predictions of a humor-free Israel were in line with this vision of a radical break with Jewish life in exile. Herzl, we recall, in his imagined version of a Jewish homeland, saw no further use for the German Jewish jokesters Gruen and Blau. The image of the native Israeli became the sabra, a local fruit sweet on the inside but prickly on the outside, signifying a toughened, even aggressive exterior. The archetypal sabra was said to lack patience for introspection, ambivalence, and the attendant neuroses that had generated Jewish humor in the past.

But *der mentsh trakht un got lakht*, a Yiddish expression whose English equivalent is "Man proposes and God disposes"—except that in the Jewish version, man proposes and God *laughs*. Once the Jewish state was actually established in 1948, both assumptions—the relation of Jewish humor to powerlessness, and the relation of statehood to power—were sorely tested. For one thing, "political normalcy" brought its own kind of limits. Before long, the Bible's description of the angels in Jacob's dream going "up and down" the ladder (Genesis 28:12) was being applied to the revolving door of Israeli immigration and emigration, the Hebrew terms for which (*aliyah* and *yeridah*) are inseparable from the moral connotation of ascent to and descent from the Land of Israel. Instructed to illustrate *aliyah* and *yeridah*, an Israeli art student drew a cartoon of Israeli schleppers hauling a sofa up the stairs of a Brooklyn home, pairing the associations of Jacob's dream with the reality that some of the student's compatriots had come to dominate a sector of the New York City moving business.

Pretty soon, the unfunny Israeli became a target of humor. The Yiddish comedians Dzigan and Schumacher, who had "ascended to" to Israel in March 1950, developed a routine in which a young officer in the Israeli army is putting a new recruit, who happens to be his own father, through morning drill:

> "You have to forget you are a father! Here, I'm your superior. We are both soldiers, and you have to follow my commands. *Hakshev*! Attention!"
>
> "Nahumke, when you want to shout at me, hold your tongue. When I was your age, you still had to wait seven years to be born. Show respect for your father!"
>
> "I'll do that at home! Here, when you hear 'hakshev,' you have to stand straight as an arrow, without batting an eye."
>
> "Oy, vey, the eggs want to be smarter than the hens."
>
> "Father, you're laughing? I'll soon have you crying like a father."[4]

The skit, which upends the ever-haunting biblical story of Abraham's binding of Isaac, spoofs the young country's attempt to impose the discipline needed for its protection. The Diaspora, represented by the father, mocks the attempt at regimentation, to which it also voluntarily submits. Yiddish balks at the superiority of Hebrew, but knows it must stop laughing and learn to soldier. The son abrogates the fifth commandment—or rather, relegates it to the home—but his threat to

Shimen Dzigan as Golda Meir. Dzigan survived the war in the Soviet Union, in prison and a labor camp. He arrived in Israel in March 1950, and his performances there adapted the irreverence he had practiced in Poland and Russia to the new Jewish state.

have his father "crying like a father" implies that he expects his parent to remain as tender toward him as ever. The Yiddish comedians use the perspective of the perpetually powerless to puncture the self-assurance of the Zionist project—of which they had become a part.

As for the expectation that Jews would no longer *need* humor to the same degree as in the past, national self-emancipation tragically failed to produce the predicted political normalcy. Hostilities against Israel increased over time, and now there was no longer any place to run to. In an older joke that had circulated from one end of wartime Europe to the other, a Jew reports having received a visa for Argentina. His friend asks, "So far away?" The Jew answers, "Far away from what?" That joke could not work in Israel, the place where Jews had come home. Thus, the second assumption about the demise of Jewish humor in an independent homeland was not only disproved but also stood on its head, as Israel became the target of the most lopsided war in history.

As it happens, there was never any real likelihood of a humorless Jewish state. Dov Sadan, the premier collector of Jewish folk speech, observed that the coming together of disparate parts of the Jewish people produced an unprecedented bounty of interethnic humor. (Sadan himself—a small man but a giant of scholarship—became known in Yiddish wordplay as a *phenomentshele.*)[5] Professional humorists who arrived in Israel as immigrants continued to ply their trade. Comedy battened on the perceived disparities between the Zionist hope—*Hatikvah*—and emergent realities. Political and social satire, censored or self-censored while Jews lived under hostile regimes, acquired a thousand new targets once Jews began running a country of their own.

After an hour of standing in line at the bank, Chaim is furious. "I hate all this waiting!" he shouts to his wife.

> "I'm leaving. I'm going to kill [Israel's first prime minister, David] Ben-Gurion."
>
> An hour later, he returns to the bank. "What happened?" asks his wife, who is still waiting in line.
>
> "Nothing," says the unhappy husband. "Over there the line was longer."[6]

Almost certainly imported from Russia, this joke tells us that Israeli joking started early and aimed right at the top. But it does not yet tell us anything about the *Jewishness* of Israeli humor.

■ Agnon, the country's most acclaimed writer, should have been able to calm from the start concerns over the prospects of Israeli humor. Born Shmuel Yosef Czaczkes in Buczacz, Galicia, Agnon ascended to the Land of Israel in 1909, left a few years later for a decade's stay in Germany, and returned to Jerusalem permanently in 1924. Developing an intricately playful way with fiction, he would forever tantalize his readers without actually handing over the key to his humor. His Hebraized name, taken from the title of his first published Hebrew story, "Agunot," invoked the figure of an agunah, an abandoned wife or unconfirmed widow who by religious law cannot be released from her marriage. Yet what did this name signify? Was he, the loyal Jew, bound to a God who had deserted but never formally divorced him, or had God died (God forbid) but without due notification? Was the resulting indeterminacy to be borne as the existential human condition, or overcome through the return to Zion or some other means? No modern Jewish writer ever drew from Jewish sources as freely or creatively as Agnon, yet as a modern artist he was always doing some mischief behind the assumed role of faithful scribe, passionate Zionist, and dignified Jew.

Shortly after the appointment of Hitler as chancellor of Germany in 1933, Agnon published *In the Heart of Seas*—a novella that perfectly demonstrates his curious amalgam of the serious and comic. The story charts the journey of a group of pious Jews from Buczacz to the Land of Israel at some unspecified time (identified by an assiduous scholar as circa 1825). Among the travelers, the author includes himself, who serves as resident storyteller to "sweeten" the trip—which may be likened to one of the roles that Agnon designed for himself within the Zionist movement. This anachronism is one of several challenges to the plain, historical-realistic level of the tale, whose characters also include Hananiah, a supernatural figure being conveyed to the homeland not in a ship but rather atop a kerchief. In brief, the voyage of a group of Jews from Europe to the Land of Israel is being accompanied by tradition (the storyteller) and faith (the name Hananiah translates as "favored by God").

Herzl had responded to the crisis of anti-Semitism in Europe by founding the Zionist movement with the exhortation *Wenn ihr wollt, ist es kein Märchen*, "If you will it, it is no fairytale." In full agreement with Herzl that Jews should reclaim their sovereignty instead of only continuing to imagine it, Agnon was nevertheless not prepared to slight the *Märchen*, without which the Jews would not have withstood the vicissitudes of exile. The book is Agnon's tongue-in-cheek rejoinder to the solemnity of Herzlian Zionism, which was in danger of tossing its cultural heritage into the heart of seas. If Jews were going to return to Zion, they would have to bring along the fruits of their exile. And if the Bible and Talmud could no longer be counted on to sustain the Jewish people, the modern writer would have to create the kind of book that would.

Agnon's answer to the challenge in this multilayered work of fiction fully admits the incongruities of modern Jewish existence as he experienced them: fealty to an inscrutable God, rights to an inaccessible homeland, and proud membership in a people everywhere vilified and threatened. The same twists and inversions that characterize the best Jewish jokes constitute the very texture of the book. Hananiah recounts how Satan, in the guise of a Polish gentleman who invites the Jew into his carriage with the command *siadaj,* once tricked him into violating the Day of Atonement. Like the traditional Jew in many earlier Jewish satires, Hananiah does not understand the language of the local population and mistakes the Polish "be seated" for the holy name for God—Shaddai. Earlier Yiddish and Hebrew satirists, in mocking such misunderstandings, were deploring the preoccupation of Jews with otherworldly matters and their consequent inability to navigate the real world. But Agnon was no longer persuaded that Polish Jews *should* accommodate themselves to their Polish surroundings. Hananiah therefore punishes himself for the opposite error: being distracted from the Jewish timetable by an invitation into a nobleman's coach.

In the Heart of Seas includes every kind of hardship and obstruction: separation from loved ones, storms at sea, sailing off course, material deprivation, and regrets and doubts that impel divorces that then require remarriages. All this is to be expected, however, for Satan is bound to interfere with what the book declares to be the ultimate Jewish commandment:

> Our men of good heart sat with their hands in their sleeves and looked out at the sea. When a man sits silent, it is assuredly a very good thing, since he is not sinning. This is particularly true when he is sitting in a ship that is going to the Land of Israel. Not only is he not sinning, but he is actually fulfilling a commandment, since he is going up to the Land of Israel; and that is a deed which is accounted as equal to the fulfillment of all the other commandments.[7]

Agnon's childlike and contrarian "proof" for the preeminence of one commandment over all others mimics rabbinic exegesis while being based on rabbinic lore. The stiff English translation tries to capture the faux piety of the style. But the ancient rabbis would hardly have designated as supreme a commandment to sit silent on an Israel-bound ship, while the pioneering Zionists who were Agnon's first readers would have seen the idealization of such a sedentary "return to Zion" as outrageous. Agnon's hyperbolic and old-style reasoning for aliyah as the ultimate value is rather like James Joyce's use of the epic grandeur of Ulysses to parody the mundane affairs of an Irish Jew.

Jewish historical memory makes for similar shipboard comedy when the women try to account for their sense of déjà vu:

> "I don't know what has come over me: for first I think that I have never seen such a lovely night, and then it

> seems to me, on the contrary, I have already seen such a night, and the very things I hear now I have heard before. I know that is not so, yet I cannot be certain it is not so."
>
> To which her companion replied, "Perhaps we have already journeyed once before to the Land of Israel, and everything we have heard and seen here we heard and saw before on some other night."
>
> "In that case," said the first, "why are we here and not in the Land of Israel?"
>
> "My dear," said the other, "we have already been there."
>
> "If we have already been there," said the first, "how is it we are here?"[8]

The circularity of this conversation—and there is more to it—may not approach Bud Abbott and Lou Costello's "Who's on First?"but its fun invites a less than reverential contemplation of the mysteries of exile and return.

Agnon's fable on the theme of returning to Zion recalls what his friend, the philosopher and scholar Scholem, said of another of his novels of this period: "Irony permeates the book from beginning to end."[9] Once the travelers settle in Jerusalem, only the fabulous character Hananiah lives and dies in a state of holiness, while the mortals meet more and less dignified ends, including at the heel of a mule and by the hand of a disgruntled Arab. Unlike Hebrew writers who tried to strip away the older, allusive layers of their language to achieve a fresh, unburdened prose, Agnon exploited the palimpsest of modernity impressed over "tradition" or tradition impressed on modernity to create fiction almost as improbable as Jewish experience.

Agnon challenged the same assumptions of progress and worldliness that his fiction did when he appeared in Stockholm in 1966 to accept the Nobel Prize for Literature from the Swedish king:

> It happened when the Swedish chargé d'affaires came and brought me the news that the Swedish Academy had bestowed the Nobel Prize upon me. Then I recited in full the blessing that is enjoined upon one who hears good tidings for himself or others: Blessed be He that is good and doeth good. "Good," in that the good God put it into the hearts of the sages of the illustrious Academy to bestow that great and esteemed Prize upon an author who writes in the sacred tongue; "that doeth good," in that He favored me by causing them to choose me. And now that I have come so far, I will recite one blessing more, as enjoined upon him who beholds a monarch: Blessed art Thou, O Lord, our God, King of the Universe, Who hast given of Thy glory to a king of flesh and blood. Over you, too, distinguished sages of the Academy, I say the prescribed blessing: Blessed be He, that has given of His wisdom to flesh and blood.[10]

In the guise of a pious and humble Jew, Agnon got across in Hebrew (switching later to English "to save the time" of translation) that he, God's delegate, was there to bestow on the monarch more than it was in the monarch's power to grant *him*. No one could have accused him of chutzpah, yet those with understanding would have understood that Agnon was pulling rank in the name of the King of kings, using his littleness to cast a shadow while showering respect on temporal authority as Jews had been doing for centuries.

At the other extreme of Agnon's subtle and erudite Hebrew humor was the *chizbat*, identified by the scholar Elliott Oring as the distinctive comic form of the Palmah, the underground army of the Jewish community in Palestine during the last years (1941–48) of the British Mandate. The Palmah (an acronym designating the "strike forces" of the Jewish militia) was made up of youngsters scarcely past adolescence who were charged with responsibility for protecting the country from increasingly violent Arab attacks and unsympathetic British overseers. The chizbat, from the Arabic for "to lie," were topical tall tales or comic stories traded around a campfire for the entertainment of fellow fighters. Their apparent artlessness may confirm, for some, the notion that the sabra had no sense of humor:

> Lulik, the squad commander of Ein ha-Horesh, was not a culture lover, but after the gang nagged him to death he agreed to lecture to them on the evolution of weapons. The fellows gathered in the tent and Lulik began, "The first man ate pistachio nuts. Then came the rifle."

Or in this alternate version:

> They came to one of the instructors, I don't remember his name, and said, "Listen. It's not possible that you teach only rifle, rifle, rifle. You need a little history, a little culture, a little sociology. You can't do with only rifle.

> Recruits come to you and you start with rifle. Start with something from the Bible . . ."
>
> He said, "O.K."
>
> When the recuits came he said, "In the beginning God created the heavens and the earth. Then came the rifle. Now this is the rifle."[11]

This new self-mockery seems fully aware of its relation to the historically layered culture to which it is opposed—and from which it emerged.

Palmahniks took inverted pride in their distance from the Talmudic scholars and intellectuals who dominated the Jewish hierarchy in bygone days. Their job was to do what Jews, for all their sophistication, were never able to do. Hence their commanders get right to the point—whether of a joke or rifle. Putting distance between themselves and the convolutions of Yiddish humor, they specialized in the kind of aggressive deflation that typifies the humor of many another nation:

> After the conquest of Eilat [in the War of Independence], Ben-Gurion arrived in the Aravah [the plain between the Dead Sea and Gulf of Aqaba] to survey the area. In every fortification they honored him with a parade, and he spoke to the soldiers. In one of the fortresses a platoon mustered for him, and Ben-Gurion, who stood on a small rise, began to prophesy: "Do you see this wilderness? There will be a forest here!"
>
> One of the guys added, "And bears will walk in it."

The cartoon figure of Srulik, diminutive of Israel, became the most recognizable representation of the sabra, the native-born Palestinian Jew, sporting the *kova tembel*, the Israeli national headgear. Created by Hungarian-born Kariel Gardosh (1921–2000), who signed himself Dosh, Srulik soldiers for the Jewish homeland, but his victories never result in the anticipated peace.

The Hebrew expression *lo dubim v'lo ya'ar* (no bears and no forest) means something like "there's nothing to it," reversing the ostensible point of Ben-Gurion's forecast. Accorded every honor as head of the country and spearhead of the war, the prime minister is mocked for a suspect species of grandiloquence that smacks of what Oring, who translated these anecdotes, calls Ben-Gurion's "extravagant prophetic vision."[12]

Idealists are not inclined to cultivate irony, and the youngsters of the Palmah were out to prove their zealotry, not their wit. Chizbat sometimes discloses familiarity with local poets (Haim Nahman Bialik or Natan Alterman) or aspects of Jewish tradition, but always in ways that discount their importance. Contrived simplicity and prideful ignorance establish a new cultural ideal, which had come to replace the Diaspora quest for hypercivilized perfection. But this phase of humor didn't last and didn't take. Following the rise of the state and establishment of an official military, some Palmahniks became professors, and some became interpreters of Agnon.

■ Neither Agnon nor chizbat figured in an eleven-part televised history of Israeli humor from before the rise of the state until its jubilee year of 1998. That is because the show covered only the fast-growing *professional* comedy of those five decades.[13] The series describes how the trickle of immigrant humorists who dominated comedy in the 1950s—such as Efraim Kishon and Dan Ben Amotz—became a tidal wave once radio spawned television, and then television as the single national channel multiplied sevenfold. Every local complaint—from the austerity and rationing of the early years to the conspicuous consumption a half century later—would eventually draw ridicule in a country whose first prime minister boasted that he governed a country of prime ministers.

The Hebrew language itself was a mainstay of comedy. Relegated for the duration of the exile to the higher regions of Jewish study, liturgy, and rabbinic correspondence, and replaced in everyday use by Jewish vernaculars that were forged wherever Jews settled for any length of time, Hebrew—the only language that could unite a people so long and so widely dispersed—experienced revival as a spoken tongue once Jews determined to reclaim their national homeland. Jokes circulated about fanatics who would not rescue a drowning person unless and until they shouted for help in the national language—and with the correct pronunciation. (As part of the move back to the East, the new speakers of Hebrew replaced its European-style pronunciation with that of its users in Arab lands.)

In the Land of Israel, German refugee professors learned Hebrew from their native-born students, Yiddish speakers were cowed into switching or silence, and Judeo-Arabic vied with local Arabic as the source of the juiciest invective and slang. On a somber note, Colonel David (Mickey) Marcus, a U.S. volunteer officer at the highest rank in the nascent Israeli army, was killed by a guard when he responded in English because he did not know the Hebrew password. But joking prospered on such misunderstandings and mistakes.

In 1953, the government of Israel established the Academy of the Hebrew Language to serve as the deciding authority on matters of grammar and terminology. If you are not laughing already, you haven't sufficiently appreciated Ben-Gurion's insight into the extravagant individualism of his fellow Israelis, who were bound to resist regimentation by their fellow Jews as vigorously as their ancestors once complied with authority imposed from without. Jews in their wanderings had already created more languages than Catholics once had children, and in Israel today you can find speakers of an estimated forty different languages. The French Academy in Paris might strive to preserve the French tongue from the inroads of Americanization (and fail even there), but an academic committee trying to influence the development of a Jewish language had as much likelihood of being heeded as an Ashkenazi referee at a soccer match attended by the largely Sephardi fans of Jerusalem Betar, the team originally founded by the Revisionist Zionist youth movement and traditionally associated with its right-wing politics.

■ This last simile was prompted by a skit, "The Judge and the Referee," by the most popular comedy team in Israel's history. If I ask an assortment of Israelis, "What comes to mind when I say, Israeli humor?" almost everyone answers "Hagashash hahiver," though a young man adds, "I don't know why I said that, since I think I've only seen one of their sketches." Improbably named "The Pale Trackers," or in shorthand, Hagashashim, the Trackers, the group made its mark in the 1960s through live performances and radio, then in the following decades on television and in films. Thanks to DVDs and YouTube, the group is accessible today at the flick of a finger.

When the Palmah was disbanded, the Israel Defense Forces that replaced it developed entertainment units as part of the military's educational program. From these dedicated amateur troupes came most of the professional entertainers in the country, including the three Gashashim: Yeshayahu "Shaike" Levi, Yisrael "Poli" Poliakov, and Gavriel "Gavri" Banai, who were tapped and trained by a talented impresario, and supplied with material by some of Israel's leading writers and lyricists.

In a society whose high culture had been shaped and dominated, if not monopolized, by Ashkenazim, the trio forged a Sephardi or Mizrahi image, maintaining distinctions in pronunciation that marked the speech of Jews from Arab lands. In the aforementioned skit, pitted against each other before a judge are a supporter of Jerusalem Betar, obviously of Middle Eastern origin, and the referee Pendelovitch, obviously of European background. The latter's offside call against Betar, which the fan had leaped on to the field to protest, was the cause of the altercation that landed the two in the courtroom. The excitable groupie is defiant and cocky; the referee is offended and petulant. Since the judge also hails from the "Eastern tribes," the advantage of common status (referee and judge are both *shofet* in Hebrew), on the one hand, is offset, on the other hand, by the advantage of common ethnicity. We wait to see which two will team up against the third, but each member of the trio is aggrieved: the intensity of the enthusiast's support for Betar has its source in the socioeconomic disadvantages of his group; the referee suffers the slings and arrows of insult along with occasional injury for trying to uphold order among savages; and the judge demands *respect* from each of the two antagonists. The three-way dispute is peppered with ethnic slurs so politically incorrect and vile that they finally reduce the referee to tears. "Don't cry," says the judge, as he approaches resolution. "I'm not the *Kotel* [the Western Wall]. Soon you'll be stuffing a petition in my ear."

The entertainment branch of the educational corps was charged with strengthening the citizenry's identification with Israel, and the Gashashim were mindful of their mis-

The Israeli comedy trio Hagashash Hahiver (The Pale Trackers) when they gained fame in the 1960s. From left to right, Shaike Levi, Poli Poliakov, Gavri Banai. Digital image of a photograph by Israel Haramati. © President and Fellows of Harvard College. From the Judaica Collection of the Harvard Library, Harvard University.

sion. They identified with the lowly against the mighty not in order to foment class conflict but rather in expectation of an eventual integration. Instead of the oppositional tension at the heart of many comic duos (Abbott and Costello, Martin and Lewis, and Dzigan and Schumacher), the trio's teamwork represented a segmented society struggling to come together, and the three actors traded places often enough to prevent any one of them from becoming the habitual butt of the others. Their ensemble approach represented the amalgamation of disparate groups under unprecedented pressures. Sociologists noted that the trio avoided divisive political issues, and used traditional and liturgical terms as well as allusions in ways that melded religion with evolving modernity so as to create an Israeli folklore that seemed drawn from the past while legitimating everything current.[14]

An example of how divisiveness becomes comic fodder for harmony is the trio's postelection skit of 1981, when the Likud Party of Menahem Begin narrowly defeated the Alignment Party of Shimon Peres. In their "morning-after" routine at a newsstand festooned with election posters, one man is reading his paper, and others come by to ask, "What are the results?" and "Can you pass me a section?" But their presumed concern with the electoral outcome turns out to be mistaken: the first man wants the score of yesterday's soccer match, and the second chews up the paper. "Hungry?" asks the owner, offering him a tastier section. The three then launch into a musical number that interprets *avodah*, the national ethic of labor, as *ovdim aleynu*, "They're Working Us Over," in which each stanza spoofs the promises made by politicians when running for office. Begin's rhetorical style is subjected to some mockery, but since the elected prime minister was heavily supported by the very underclass that the Gashashim purported to represent, the comedic trio could not indulge the kind of dismissive satire of the Israeli Right that would characterize later comedians appealing to the country's left-of-center elites. The song's refrain, "They're working us over . . . and we never learn," was inherently democratic.

In its shows, the trio indulged in some slapstick and masquerading, but in typical Jewish fashion specialized in language and wit: a fitting area for humor in a new land where philosophers and flower sellers, mechanics and kibbutzniks, were caught up alike in the insecurities of an emerging language. Indeed, the committee awarding the Israel Prize to the Gashashim in 2000 singled out these comedians' contribution to the language while several times invoking the term "loving" to describe the nature of their impact on Israeli culture, society, and state. The commendation read: "Anyone who wants to know who we were and what we did in the first half-century of the State of Israel may turn to the work of the Gashashim."[15] (In regard to the trio's YouTube rendition of "*ovdim aleynu,*" viewers remark on how little has changed in the intervening years.)

■ Yet if we were to trace Israel's history through its humor, we would perceive a downward trajectory in precisely those qualities of courtesy, affection, and national cohesion that the Israel Prize committee remarked on in its praise of the Gashashim. Their own later humor, indeed, would become coarsened with features that seemed to be coarsening the culture at large, in part thanks to the ambiguous consequences of rising standards of living. In a skit titled "Kreker vs. Kreker"—a takeoff on the 1979 U.S. film *Kramer vs. Kramer*—a family argument erupts among a wealthy husband, wife, and only child in which the escalating exchanges of invective resemble those that once raged between the fan and referee in the earlier skit, except that the impersonated female buffing her nails in contempt of her husband is far less charming than the Betar enthusiast who cannot restrain his love for his team. The cooling attachment of wife for husband reflects the cooling affection of her social class for the family of Israel, and a society once comical for its difficulties in coming together is now mocked for its ease in coming apart. The drugs and depression that eventually took their toll on some of those who wrote for the Gashashim left their mark on the country's humor as well.

But the most obvious cause for the darkening colors of Israeli humor was, and remains, the regional hostility that overturned the nation's expectations of political normalcy. Of all the predictions of Zionism, none was as severely thwarted as the prospect of peaceful relations between the Jewish state and its neighbors. Liberal democracies are by nature reluctant combatants, and Jews, who had long since developed a politics of accommodation to power, realized only slowly and reluctantly that in Israel, winning wars might remain the necessary price of Jewish survival.

Israel's first feature film, *Hill 24 Doesn't Answer* (1955), remains—despite its English and polyglot dialogue—the most iconic representation of Israel's War of Independence. Its conventional story line shows four soldiers of varied backgrounds and languages trying to secure a strategic outpost against superior Arab forces that also include a former unrepentant Nazi. The sacrifice of the few secures the land for the many. In a 1975 parody of this film starring the Gashashim, *Hill Halfon Doesn't Answer*, a sergeant in love with the younger daughter of a certain Victor Hasson has been ordered to bring back to his outpost in the Sinai an Italianate Israeli gambler named Sergio Konstanza, who is hoping to elude his Egyptian Israeli creditor, the said Hasson. Although the post's soldiers and commanding officer are presumably concerned about an impending Egyptian attack, slapstick routines with exploding grenades and bulldozed outdoor privies make ostentatious fun of the enterprise. Funniest is the dialogue, here between a visiting commander and Hasson, who has come to the post in pursuit of his prey and must pretend that he, too, is doing military service.

> "What do you do if the Egyptians approach the post?"
> "What we did in '56!"
> "What did you do in '56?"
> "What we did in '48. It doesn't get better than that!"
> "What did you do in '48?"
> "Thirty years ago, you expect me to remember?"[16]

Lampooning the disparity between a determinedly informal citizenry and the demands of military exigency, the parody also acknowledges that the War of Independence is still being fought. And in fact, by the time of this film, in addition to the wars of 1956 and 1948, Israel had been made to fight the war of 1967, the 1969–70 "war of attrition" along the Suez Canal, and the Yom Kippur War of 1973. Yet when Hasson accidentally crosses a UN boundary, is picked up by the Egyptians, and interrogated as a spy, the episode is played not only for laughs but also for laughs at the very idea that there is any real enmity involved. Hasson teaches his Arab interrogator, a fellow "Mizrahi," how to make proper coffee, and prisoner and interrogator even sing a line or two together from *Fiddler on the Roof* in a salute to the international culture that embraces all.[17]

Some of Israel's war-weary humor can be likened to that of the U.S. movie and long-running sitcom *MASH* (1970,

1972–83), which transformed the Korean battlefront, at a distance of twenty years, into a theater of comedy. The antiwar sting of *MASH* reflected the political outlook of Americans opposed to their country's military role in Vietnam, suggesting the absurdities of the current involvement through the supposed absurdities of the earlier one. *Halfon*, the Gashashim version of this antiwar comedy, was existentially (though perhaps not artistically) more complex, since the enemy was within arm's reach, and no Jew in the country was exempt from the fight.

This paradoxically may help to explain why *Halfon* has become a staple of Israel Independence Day entertainment, whereas replaying a film like *Hill 24 Doesn't Answer* would merely reopen the wound of unrealized hopes—hopes that had been an integral element of the Jewish struggle for historical vindication. Rehearsing an ironic response to those unrealized hopes is a way of reaffirming Israel's resolution to carry on precisely in the face of disappointed expectations. In the way that Yiddish comedy seldom portrayed the main cause of its anxiety, but instead sought comic relief in intramural ridicule that obscured the greater enemy threat, *Halfon* obscures the real and present Arab danger through spoofs of incompetent Jews. The Israeli army post has replaced Sholem Aleichem's railroad car as the place where threatened Jews come comically together.

The heyday of the Gashashim and *Hill Halfon Doesn't Answer* coincided with a period of relative optimism in Israel, but the diplomatic assault on the country's legitimacy and expanding menace of terrorism gradually hardened the national sense of siege. Even Anwar Sadat's welcome visit in 1977 took away with one hand what it brought with the other, requiring Israel's traumatic withdrawal from the Sinai and a treaty that never yielded the reciprocal relations it promised. That the formal peace concluded between the two countries caused Egypt's expulsion from the Arab League and triggered Sadat's assassination two years later reinforced not Egypt's but Israel's isolation, since it showed the depth of pan-Arab commitment to the war against the Jewish state. Moreover, once Egypt made it clear that it had no intention of honoring the terms of the agreement it had undertaken, it was allowed back into the League.

Why drag the war against Israel into a book on Jewish humor? Because Jewish humor is affected by anti-Jewish politics. Like salt poured into water, unwelcome hostility turns Jewish humor more flavorful yet progressively heavier. Seeking acceptance from their opponents, some Jews have always expressed the frustrations of their unrequited goodwill through humor. Greater enmity from without increases the wish for comic relief from the indignity of having to suffer the consequences of another people's madness. One might call it a psychochemical reaction with by now predictable results, which is why students of Israeli humor single out January 16–18, 1991, at the height of the first Gulf War, as its most significant turning point to date.[18] The rain of Scud missiles that brought the conflict to noncombatant Israel gave new meaning to the depiction of Tel Aviv as "the city that never sleeps."

The missile raids of the first Gulf War were distinguished from previous Arab attacks not by the toll in casualties, which were comparatively light, but instead by the imposed proscription of acts of self-defense. Arab member states included in the coalition that the United States led against Saddam Hussein to prevent his annexation of Kuwait refused to allow Israel's "participation" even when the country came under direct attack. This caused the absurd spectacle of Israelis huddling in sealed rooms with gas masks because their allies, the Americans, did not allow them to strike back against the common Iraqi foe—a foe whose Arab connections permitted it to bombard the Jews without fear of retaliation by them. No less convoluted was the U.S. effort to intercept and shoot down Hussein's Scuds lest Israelis be killed as a consequence of the United States having prevented their self-defense. The absurdist twists of Heller's *Catch-22* (an antiwar novel originally written with a Jewish rather than Armenian protagonist) seem puny by comparison.

No Israeli parent, having donned and helped his or her children into gas masks, could fail to recognize a resemblance to the situation of the gassed Jews of Europe—a situation that the Israeli's own parents may have escaped, or that their grandparents had come to Israel to avoid. The army spokesperson who reported the news during this war was dubbed *Tilim Zoger*: *tilim* is Hebrew for "missiles," and *tehilim zoger* is Yiddish for the psalm-reciting functionary whom traditional Jews relied on to secure divine protection. Psychologists concluded that "when Jews in Israel were confronted with conditions similar to those in the Diaspora, the characteristics of old Jewish humor appeared again."[19] Israelis themselves made the connection: "What's the difference between Saddam and Haman [the archetypal villain of the Book of Esther and the Jewish masquerading holiday of Purim]? Haman was hanged, and then we donned masks. With Saddam, the masks came first."

The humiliations of enforced passivity were augmented by the televised display of Palestinians dancing on their rooftops at the sight of missiles falling on Israeli Jews—and on fellow Arabs. Israeli identity, forged in opposition to the political impotence of the Diaspora, was confronted with a political experience almost designed to prove a historical connection between the two conditions.

■ But that is only one part, and the grimmer part, of Israeli humor in those days. If some joking flowed back into more familiar Jewish channels—including the preference for internalized humor versus humor directed at the enemy—this was less true of the humor under active development by the Mizrahi Jews of Israel, whose presence had by then affected all aspects of the country's formal and popular culture. Just as the specifically European forms of anti-Semitism were alien to Jews deriving from Arab lands, so it was commonly observed, these Jews had also been bypassed by the European "Enlightenment" with its consequent separation of church from state. In part as a result, they tended to feel more at ease with religious observance than did many of their Ashkenazi counterparts, and less threatened by a politicized rabbinate.

All this may help to account for the popularity of one of Israel's comic creations that came into its element during the first Gulf War: the Baba Buba, fashioned after the renowned

Baba Sali (Yisrael Abuhatzeira, 1890–1984, rabbi and kabbalist who had spearheaded the emigration of Moroccan Jewry to Israel) and his son Baba Borukh, who still played a key role among Israel's Mizrahi Jews. The honorific *baba* is Arabic for "father," and *buba* (rhymes with tuba) is Hebrew for "doll," telegraphing Baba Buba's parodic function as a cartoonlike authority dispensing interpretations of current events with all the acumen of Gilda Radner's news commentator Roseanne Roseannadanna on *Saturday Night Live*.

Baba Buba's tool of interpretation was *gematria*, which makes use of the numerical value of Hebrew letters to ascribe hidden meaning to words and expressions. The custom had a respectable rabbinic history, but its apparent irrationality had made it a target of Jewish satire from the beginning of the nineteenth century. Enacted by the comic Moni Moshonov, Baba Buba interprets events in the news by subjecting them to the methods of gematria embellished with absurd exegeses of people's names—for instance, by reversing the elements that make up the name Schwartzkopf ("Blackhead," after Norman Schwartzkopf, commander of the coalition forces in the war), because "only after things happen do we know what should have happened to begin with."[20] In a study of the psychological contributions of humor to Israel during this crisis, Ofra Nevo suggests that such reversals and paradoxes were an ideal vehicle for the irrational process people were experiencing. The logic of gematria was less kooky than that of requiring Israel to play sitting target in order to accommodate Arab nations that could not fight their own battles.

Of course, in Israel as elsewhere, the nature and quality of humor are governed as much by professional opportunities and technological innovation as by the historical and cultural conditions I have been describing. A 1983 law permitting commercial television channels to break the state's monopoly brought on the kind of comedy glut that suffuses television in the United States.

Israel's most popular humor revue, *Eretz Nehederet* (A wonderful country), often compared with *Saturday Night Live*, resembles its prototype in producing weekly shows on a regular schedule—unlike the Gashashim who perfected and refined their routines as if for the theater. The result is an artistically uneven record, with sometimes-loutish comedy receiving the heartiest laughs from the live audience—probably no different from the norm in Shakespeare's day. By loutish I mean a bar mitzvah boy playing with his penis as the MC announces that the lad has his speech in hand, or a flamboyant U.S. blond, played by a cross-dressed male actor, outcursing the Israeli cowboy trying to pick her up. On the political scale the show tips leftward, and instinctively favors Mizrahim when they come up against Ashkenazim in the same way that *Saturday Night Live* stays politically correct when it treats the racial divide between blacks and whites. But an Israeli niche market has also developed for right-wing comedy that mocks the very talk show hosts and broadcasters who try to take down the Likud prime minister. For instance, on the Latma Web site, the "reporter"—typecast as a candidate for Conservatives Anonymous—conducts interviews on the Yom Kippur War with actors playing an Egyptian Islamist and Israeli leftist, neither of who can bring themselves to admit that Israel fought the war to victory.

"Sometimes things here are so surreal we have to laugh at them," says one of the writers of *Eretz Nehederet*. Yet in confronting the elements that make life "surreal," many of those in the business of *Israeli* comedy are reluctant to see the connection between earlier *Jewish* humor and theirs. Much as Bellow and Roth flaunted their Jewish origin yet balked at being labeled as Jewish writers, creators of comedy in Israel freely admit their indebtedness to the United States but are skittish about their Jewish affinities. When I tell a couple of fans of *Eretz Nehederet* that I am studying the Jewish humor of Israel, they are taken aback, protesting that there is no Jewish humor in Israel. This reminds me of the banker Otto Kahn, who had converted to Christianity. Walking along the street one day with a hunchbacked friend, he passed a synagogue and confided, "You know, I used to be a Jew." The friend replies, "And I used to be a hunchback."

And Molière's Monsieur Jourdain did not know he was speaking prose.

▪ In 1988, a year before the sitcom *Seinfeld* was launched on U.S. television, the Israeli actor Shmuel Vilozhny produced a modest documentary film that used the same dramatic device of alternating between a comedy-club routine and the real-life situation on which the routine is based. *Abaleh, kah oti l'luna park*, translated as "Daddy, take me to the fair," a line echoing a Hebrew popular song of the 1930s, is based on a trip that Vilozhny took to Poland in the company of his father and younger sister. In an opening monologue in the comedy club, Vilozhny describes his family of Holocaust survivors. It seems that there is a constant feud between his father, who refuses to buy any German-made products, and his uncle, who buys nothing but German-made products on the grounds that German goods are the best. How does he know they are the best? The uncle rolls up his sleeve to boast that the camp number engraved on his arm "never comes off."

This wins a laugh from the audience. Vilozhny evokes the strained relations between sabra-son and survivor-father in a tone that assumes his listeners share his impatience with the genocide that darkened their parents' lives—and consequently, theirs. The comedian seems almost surly as he accompanies his father back "home": "My only concern is that you'll start speaking Polish." The footage of the trio at the start of their voyage captures the discomfort of all involved.

There are by now dozens of accounts of young people tracing their familial roots in eastern Europe, with or without their parents; Vilozhny's footage of his own family's visit to Auschwitz includes a tour group of young Jews on a similar pilgrimage. But in the way that comedy punctures factuality, what goes on between son and father breaks through the standard features of this journey with its obligatory visit to native town, family home, and intended final destination. At the heart of *this* film is a scene where Vilozhny senior describes how, as a boy, he would use fallen tree branches to play at dueling. Shmuel goes looking, and soon enough father and son have begun to fence, with the father teaching his son the rudiments of parry and thrust until they go at it for real, and the viewer starts to worry lest the game end in symbolic patricide or filicide. As the daughter observes, though, the sparring actually achieves the opposite effect, bringing each a momentary taste of the carefree childhood that only the father had ever truly experienced. The pressure of trying to spare his children the knowledge of what he had endured before becoming their Israeli parent had raised a wall of silence between the generations. Now they are convulsed in laughter, released by swordplay instead of wordplay.

The town record book, which the family later consults, serendipitously reveals that the father is several years younger than he had thought—as if confirming what he had gained by introducing his children to his past. Conversely, Shmuel's reaction to being at Auschwitz is to "want to stay silent for eternity." The catharsis that releases spontaneous familial laughter allows this voluble comedian to be still.

Abaleh, kah oti l'luna park broke through prohibitions about using the Shoah for comedy even as it deepened connections with the Jewish past. The child's reference to his father in the diminutive—Daddy, rather than Dad—expresses this intimacy, with the Yiddish suffix yoking the Hebrew/Israeli noun to its Jewishness. To appreciate this accord, we need only think of the bitter letter written by Kafka to *his* father, and his even more haunting reflection that "I did not always love my mother as she deserved and as I could, only because the German language prevented it. The Jewish mother is no '*Mutter*,' to call her '*Mutter*' makes her a little comic."[21] The term *Vater*, too, is far from meaning the Jewish father, which leaves Kafka fatally and essentially alienated from his parents.

For Kafka, the tragic component of life was less the threat from the Germans as enemy—though he takes full account of that as well—than the degree to which a foreign language had prevented what, in opposition, the Vilozhnys of the world have been able to forge. It is possible that Israeli immigrant parents were inhibited from speaking "freely" with their children as much by having to do so in an adopted language as by the trauma they hoped to suppress; this would give Jewish-style comedy and a Yiddishized Hebrew special importance in binding the generations—as happens in this film. The fact is that Shmuel's father could not have taken his children on a trip with a happier outcome, or so his children have chosen to interpret it.

Vilozhny's embrace of the Shoah coincided with an upsurge of interest in the subject on the part of his generation that did not always result in the wry brand of Jewish humor he practices. By way of contrast, the writer David Grossman's influential novel *See Under: Love*, published almost simultaneously with the release of Vilozhny's film, elevated the trauma of an Israeli child doomed merely to imagine the Nazi beast above the trauma of those actually devoured by the beast in Europe. Despite concerted attempts by Israel's leaders and cultural figureheads to reduce the traumatic aftereffects of the European genocide—among other ways, by emphasizing the dynamic potential of newly won political autonomy—survivors who reached Israel could not help but wish to record what they had witnessed, to memorialize the dead, and call for collective as well as individual mourning. The establishment in 1953 of Yad Vashem as a "living memorial to the Holocaust" and the trial of Adolf Eichmann in Jerusalem in 1961 gave national expression to the attempts of citizens to cope with the losses as well as shocks that they had sustained. The Shoah cast a long, dark shadow over the country that had defied probability in its buoyant birth and development; many children of Israel's pioneers and Europe's refugees alike resented the burdens of history they were expected to bear.

Yet Vilozhny was not alone in using humor to come to terms with an unwelcome past. Something even livelier occurs in Amir Gutfreund's novel *Shoah shelanu* (Our Holocaust, 2001), an alternately heavy and lighthearted representation of Israelis who voluntarily assume the role of "grandchildren" of those who left no biological issue. Also a child of Polish refugees, the author creates a narrator who is removed enough from the unspeakable horrors experienced by survivors to investigate the ironies inherent in that term.

> Grandpa used to say, "People have to die of something," and refused to donate to the war against cancer, the war against traffic accidents, or any other war. To avoid being considered stingy, he would occasionally burst into exemplary displays of tremendous generosity. He put on these shows with such proficiency that if not for us, his relatives, no one would have known the simple truth: he was a miser.[22]

The children of those who came out of Europe had to piece together events that their elders were loath to describe, and determine what was theirs to avenge, redeem, or ignore. So, too, the narrator has to figure out the relative influences of inborn character and historical impact—nature and nurture—in the formation of those who surround him. Gutfreund's narrator explains that his family's Law of Compression was a wonderful invention of those who, "lacking brothers, uncles, fathers, and mothers, had done away with the requirement for precision," and adopted as family anyone with a corresponding wish for adoption.[23] Because "Grandpa" is not his actual progenitor, the narrator can expose his foibles without an offspring's rancor and figure out at his own pace where he stands in relation to his intriguingly quirky, murky inheritance. Gutfreund, himself a lieutenant colonel in the Israeli air force, saw no contradiction between his twin careers as officer and master of ironic fiction.

▪ Jewish humor remains, as it always has been, merely one of many possible responses to the anomalous experience of the Jews. But as long as it does remain one of those responses, suppliers will arise to meet the demand. Some of Israel's most talented and popular writers—Meir Shalev, Haim Beer, and Etgar Keret—have developed individual styles of humor that stand at a philosophical remove from the exigencies of everyday life in the Jewish state. On my table are stacked books on Israeli humor, articles about Israeli humor, articles and books by Israelis on the humor of other nations, videos and DVDs of Israeli comedians and Israeli comedies, and assorted cartoons and clippings attesting to this comedy surge. One of Israel's premier publishers recently issued a selection of anecdotes and jokes from a three-volume treasury collected by Alter Druyanov, who after his arrival in Palestine in 1922, anthologized Hebrew translations of Jewish humor, mostly from Yiddish.

The editor and illustrator of the new volume of selections, the artist Danny Kerman, writes that Druyanov's collections, the only books that his generation of Israelis needed no encouragement to read, informed his contemporaries' idea of humor, period.

And since comedy relies on immediate feedback, humor in Israel does have to satisfy Jews who constitute over three-quarters of the population. Joking depends on what the audience knows and feels. Israeli humor perforce plays on what Jews undergo. Some of the sharpest Jewish humor will keep bubbling up from below, letting the professionals know when a target is ripe for lampooning and when a boil has to be lanced. At least as long as Israel is the main target of Israel's enemies, it will remain an incubator of Jewish humor.

During the Second Intifada—the orchestrated suicide bombings of the 1990s that were Israel's reward for the Oslo Peace Accords—a Jerusalem relative told me a joke she had heard that had "everyone rolling on the floor":

> Sara in Jerusalem hears on the news about a bombing at a popular café near the home of relatives in Tel Aviv. She calls in a panic and reaches her cousin, who assures her that thankfully, the family is all safe.
>
> "And Anat?" Sara asks after the teenager whose hang-out it had been.
>
> "Oh, Anat," says her mother, reassuringly, "Anat's fine. She's at Auschwitz!"

As against those who would object to the joke's insensitivity or fail to understand it, the Israelis who laughed share a certain knowledge and sensibility. They know that as part of their education, Israeli teenagers are routinely taken on trips to Poland that include visits to the death camps where some of their ancestors perished. They may have felt a little queasy joking about the Holocaust, and such residual qualms would account for the *explosive* hilarity that comes with breaking taboos. The joke crosses the wires of anxiety over Jew-killing past and present, and revels in the forced recognition—surprise of surprises—that today's danger may be greater than yesterday's. It reassures us that the sense of "horror" spoken of by Reik persists in the recovered homeland. By acknowledging the infamous Nazi death camp as a refuge from what was intended to be the Jewish place of refuge, the joke offends both sides of the political spectrum—liberals who deny the ferocity of Arab aggression, and patriots who cannot acknowledge that Zionism does not fully safeguard the Jews.

The joke's reputation as a sidesplitter prompted me to tell it one evening to a pair of Israeli friends, Michael and Ruth Rabin, who spend part of every year in Cambridge, Massachusetts. Michael is a pioneer theorist of computer science, and Ruth a former judge; both are connoisseurs and superb practitioners of the art of joke telling. But neither laughed—a response so unusual in our habitual repartee that it seemed to call for an explanation. Michael broke the awkward silence that follows an unappreciated joke with this counteroffering: "We used to say that there were two kinds of German Jews: the pessimists who went to Palestine, and the optimists who went to Auschwitz." A child of the pessimists, he drew for his punch line on the unwelcome, long-resisted, politically improbable, yet ultimately comforting realization that security in Zion was more plausible than the once-assured comforts of Europe.

Both jokes end on the same word, but the mature Israelis' failure to laugh at its later version (unless I told the joke badly, or it lacked the punch in Cambridge that it would have had in Jerusalem) suggests that it may take longer than a lifetime for Jews to appreciate wit at the expense of their own formative assumptions of what Jewish humor is all about. Do you know the joke about the Polish comedian who boasts that the key to his talent is "t . . . t . . . t . . . timing"? The same principle holds true for humor at large. At a generation's remove, Syrkin and Scholem could not appreciate Roth. Humor is delimited by chronology as much as by culture and language.

Conclusion

When Can I Stop Laughing?

This is not the place to examine why I, a Jew, feel more threatened by those who would wipe out ethnic jokes than by those who unthinkingly make them. But it may be the place simply to record that I do.

—Howard Jacobson, *Seriously Funny*

History itself seems to be making fun of the Jewish tourist in Europe who now pays good money for an excursion to the Auschwitz death camp or for a ticket to see Prague's Pinkas Synagogue, whose walls are inscribed with the names of 77,297 murdered Czech Jews. Nothing in the works of Kafka is quite as weird as the presence of *two* competing Kafka museums in the city where he once imagined the hero of his novel *The Trial* being slaughtered "like a dog," with only his shame to outlive him.

Nor is history's mockery confined to Jews. On a recent trip to Prague with a Catholic friend who was born in the city, she and I stayed at a cozy hotel that, as it turned out, had been converted from a police station—the very place where her mother had been interrogated when her father, a Czech patriot, fled the Communists in 1948. Yesterday's tortures had become today's conveniences, inviting us both to enjoy the ironies of our respective good fortunes. Of course, because Jewish suffering has lately trumped its Christian counterparts in Europe, Jewish kitsch wins out over its competitors; in Prague, many more images of Kafka than of the Czech religious martyr Jan Hus grace tourist posters and matchboxes.

In one of the obligatory gift shops of Prague's six refurbished synagogues, from among the *tchatchkes* and postcards I picked up a glossy paperback titled *Jewish Anecdotes from Prague* that I anticipated would contain legends of the golem—the figure fashioned from clay and allegedly brought to life by the sixteenth-century rabbi Judah Loew to protect the city's Jews from impending attack. The legend is there, to be sure, but the Czech author of the book, Vladimir Karbusicky, a distinguished musicologist in his professional life, is more interested in the stories of his own time than in those of the distant past. A native of the city, he has collected the jokes of the Jews who formed about 20 percent of its population before the Second World War because he associates the city's magic with their form of humor. The legend of the golem reminds him of the following anecdote that circulated before the Second World War:

> Leopold Munk has died. Always cheerful, healthy, ruddy, and suddenly . . . he has simply died. The family gathers around him, weeping and wailing. Into the room comes a certain Krauskopf [Curlyhead] who wants to know what is going on.

"Don't ask! Leopold Munk has died."

"Died? How?"

"Just like that."

"Nonsense," says Krauskopf, "I'll resurrect him. Bring me a glass of wine."

Given the wine, Krauskopf raises the glass and calls, "Leopold, to your health!" He downs the wine, but there is no response from the deceased.

Krauskopf shakes his head and says, "Bring me stronger wine. This was too weak." They bring it and he calls in a louder voice: "Leopold, to your health. Arise!" But the dead man lies still.

The request for stronger wine is repeated once or twice more, until they bring Krauskopf the strongest wine. He drinks it and roars: "Leopold, I say: To your health! You are supposed to get up!"

Leopold Munk doesn't rise.

Krauskopf looks thoughtfully at the deceased and then says in admiration: "Now that's what I call dead!"[1]

Death is a common subject of jokes, thereby feeding on our common anxieties, and humor normally sides with mortals who enjoy the advantages of life at the expense of the deceased. Serving up these old jokes, the author seems painfully aware that he may resemble the freeloader by benefiting from his own doomed attempts to resurrect the dead who told these jokes and savored this brand of humor. Indeed, the book itself, like the nostalgia on which the city's tourism relies, suggests that all of Prague nowadays profits from a version of Krauskopf's necromancy.

The Talmud's most popular tractate, Pirkei Avot (The wisdom of the fathers), teaches that "whoever cites his source by name brings deliverance to the world." The rabbis honored not only the teaching that was passed down through generations but also the integrity of the process of transmission. In a similar act of homage, Karbusicky recounts this anecdote in the name of its teller, the popular Jewish humorist and cabaret entertainer Karel Polacek (1892–1945), who had performed it as part of his repertoire.

Polacek the Jew was taken to the Terezin concentration camp in 1943, and from there to his death in Auschwitz; at about the same time, Karbusicky the Christian was sent as a slave laborer to Hamburg. When Karbusicky returned to Prague, by then under Soviet rule, he found employment in the Ethnographic Institute of the Czechoslovak Academy of Sciences. He collected Jewish anecdotes as part of his work, though their "antiauthoritarian" disposition made it prudent to keep them under lock and key. Forced to emigrate in 1969 (he found refuge in West Germany), he had to leave the humor collection behind, and was never thereafter able to retrieve it. He thus reconstructed this collection from memory and other anthologies, publishing it as homage to former Jewish classmates who went missing in Auschwitz. Macabre motifs, he points out, characterized Jewish joking long before the Holocaust.

The many jokes in Karbusicky's collection, interchangeable with others across east-central Europe, may not prove his contention that "nowhere are such fine Jewish anecdotes told as in Prague," yet they remain his touchstone of an "authentic" Prague culture that reached its apogee in the interwar years.[2] They connect him to the liberal tradition that is threatened in his region by repressive forces on the political Left and Right. The spunk of these jokes achieves some of the freedom that their tellers could not. The following one dates from after the war, from the four decades of Communist rule, enforced by Soviet rulers from 1948 until the Velvet Revolution of the late 1980s.

> Mr. Roubitschek [a mainstay of Czech Jewish joking] has done so well in the [Communist] Ministry of Commerce that they've sent him to Budapest to negotiate a new contract for the exchange of goods. The next day a telegram comes: "Contract successfully negotiated—stop—Long Live Free Hungary!"
>
> This pleases the Minister, so Roubitschek is sent to Warsaw. On the third day, a telegram arrives: "Contract successfully negotiated—stop—Long Live Free Poland!"
>
> Roubitschek's enthusiasm for the freedom of the socialist system wins the political trust of his superiors. He is ceremoniously summoned: "Comrade Roubitschek! You speak many languages and will therefore be given the important mission of negotiating a treaty for us in the West."
>
> Mr. Roubitschek packs his bags and sets out. A week later a telegram comes to the Ministry. "Am in Paris—

> stop—business going well—stop—Long live Free Roubitschek!"[3]

Like the joke about diabetes with which this book began, this one likewise turns on the double meaning of a term—with the Jew here winning release from the repressive system that he has been obediently hailing as "free." He can finally release truth from the lies that he has been compelled to repeat.

But what do these liberating anecdotes gain from having been ascribed to Jews? One can readily see why *Jews* might give their jokes a Jewish coloration, but why did non-Jews ascribe a Jewish provenance to anecdotes that could as easily have circulated about Catholic Czechs, or in Poland about Catholic Poles? Why continue to use recognizably Jewish names like Munk, Krauskopf, and Roubitschek if these jokes are being told in Czech, and might just as well have been told with Czech protagonists? Why did the Jewishness of Jewish joking gain ecumenical appeal under repressive regimes?

It seems that as long as Jews experienced intimidation, repression, and terror aimed at them specifically, their humor held little attraction for onlookers who wanted to stay clear of the fray. Once fascism and Communism routed and regimented the rest of the population as well, though, Jewish humor resonated with citizens under similar attack, and became emblematic of the kind of freedom that "Roubitschek" personifies. For staunch liberals like Karbusicky—and his counterparts in other subjugated countries of Europe—Jewish anecdotes acted much like Winston Churchill's V for Victory sign—the two-fingered gesture used by the British prime minister throughout the Second

World War to signal the eventual triumph of a humanized Europe. The Czech liberal emphasizes the Jewishness of his joking because where liberalism is under siege, the Jewish joke stands for independence, for the right to joke and freedom to mock.

Karbusicky's book of Jewish anecdotes brings us full circle from Samantha, the Harvard secretary I discussed at the beginning of this book who feared Jewish joking because it *offended* her generous humanism. I now arrive at the musicologist who embraces Jewish joking because it *exemplifies* that same generous impulse. There is an irony in the fact that the Czech welcomes the kind of laughter the United States fears. Samantha's idea of tolerance was shaped in the aftermath of the civil rights movement, which worked so hard to eliminate stereotyping that it left its loyal adherents nervous about any ethnic joke whatsoever. For the Czech Karbusicky, the very presence of a differentiated citizen—and perhaps the Jew in particular—defies the uniformity of the robotic subjects whom totalitarian regimes have tried to create and rule. For him, Jewish joking is proof of this creative defiance. He has lived under Communism; she has not. He has shared the Jew's fate; she has not. He would probably have roared at the joke about diabetes and added it to his collection; she worries lest mockery seduces us into accepting what we ought to resist.

■ As this book nears its end, some readers may still question the impulse to separate one culture from another rather than finding and celebrating their commonalities. Others may impatiently await a definition of Jewish humor that will distinguish it once and for all from Gentile varieties. To them all I would say that the distinction lies more in the Jews' greater reliance on humor than in the precise nature of that humor. A reduced nation with a magnified image exploits the paradoxes of being an "ever-dying people," as the scholar Simon Rawidowicz called the Jews. An exegetical tradition that values literate intelligence cultivates wit as one of its values, and a religious tradition of great self-restraint seeks permissible forms of self-expression. A culture forged in the ancient East that developed in the modern West, and a theology founded in divine election whose adherents have been targeted for genocide—such incongruities tickle the modern Jewish imagination. These are among the reasons for the proliferation of humor among Jews.

Freud sought freedom not from the repression imposed by Nazis and Soviets but rather from the restraints of Jewish civilization itself, which some, including Freud himself, have equated with bourgeois civility in general. He believed that persons "might be willing to renounce all the methods of satisfaction forbidden by society if only they could be certain that in return society will reward this renunciation by offering them permitted methods of satisfaction." Freud personally sought some of that satisfaction in cigars and cocaine, but joking offered him headier release as part of a group. In a poignant passage, he confides that such satisfaction may not only be desirable but also *necessary*: "What these jokes whisper may be said aloud: that the wishes and desires of men have a right to make themselves acceptable alongside of exacting and ruthless morality."[4] For those Jews who submit to the compounded constraints of their own arduous civilizing regimen and their requisite adjustment to Gentile majorities, the attribution of *ruthlessness* to morality rings especially true. Joking becomes their bid for freedom, if only through the utterance of otherwise-prohibited truth.

Yet as the crowing of roosters and barking of dogs are transcribed variously in every alphabet, Jewish humor changes with language and circumstance. By dividing this book's chapters according to language and political region, I have tried to show that Jews joke differently in Yiddish than in English, differently among themselves than in the presence of non-Jews, and differently in constitutional democracies than in totalitarian states. When Heine quipped, "Wie es sich christelt, so jüdelt es sich"—"as go the Christians, so go the Jews"—he was making fun of the latter's overenthusiastic Europeanization. When a century later, George S. Kaufman punned, "One man's Mede is another man's Persian," he was appropriating a maxim about individual taste ("One man's meat is another man's poison") to make the lighter point that cultural differences exist in name only: Medes *are* Persians. The acidity of Heine's German aphorism contrasts with the sweetness of the U.S. pun, but typical of both men is their delight in the cross-cultural wordplay. What they most have in common is not the content of their wit but rather their reliance on wit.

■ Vagaries of Jewish Humor

To be honest, there was a time when I too might have tried to identify some essentials of Jewish humor that distinguish it from other comic traditions. For example, I once scanted slapstick, rating the verbalizing Marx Brothers much higher than the physically antic Three Stooges—and in the comedy of the former troupe, Groucho's puns and double entendres higher than the elaborate pieces of visual hilarity like the stateroom scene in *Night at the Opera* or mirror scene in *Duck Soup*. I thought of slapstick as a Gentile specialty, a respite from the cerebral anxieties of Jewish joking. As my gold standard of Gentile humor, I took the "Make 'Em Laugh" routine in the 1952 musical *Singin' in the Rain*, in which Donald O'Connor treats his body as a mannequin of movable parts, perfectly illustrating Henri Bergson's view of comedy as "something mechanical encrusted on the living."[5] As if to prove my point about the nature of its Gentile appeal, when the writers of the 2007 television series *Mad Men* conjured up the archetypal Protestant American suburban housewife of the 1950s, they imagined *Singin' in the Rain* as her favorite movie.

In fact, physical comedy did come later and slower to Jews than the cerebral and literary kind. Ancient Greek comedy and its imitators featured slapstick and bawdy humor that is nowhere celebrated in the ancient Jewish texts. In the Middle Ages, the precarious political arrangements of Jewish communities in Christian lands damped the carnival spirit that was periodically loosed all around them and that occasionally expressed its riotousness at the Jews' expense. In modern times, legal suppression in czarist Russia retarded the development of the start-up Yiddish theater, and staging inhibitions may have contributed to keeping it more verbal than physical. When Yiddish theater did erupt in London and New York at the end of the nineteenth century, its most popular entertainer was the nimble improviser Zelig Mogulescu—until fashion changed and melodrama challenged comedy, forcing Mogulescu to memorize his lines.

But once Jews hit vaudeville and the movies, they swung for the fences, and their physical shtick competed with the best. To test this proposition, interrupt your reading of this paragraph to watch (on YouTube) the climactic scene of *The Court Jester*, and ask which is funnier—Kaye attempting to memorize "the pellet with the poison's in the vessel with the pestle; the chalice from the palace has the brew that is true" or Kaye poking his head out of his beheaded suit of armor in his joust to the death with the gigantic Sir Griswold. The physically challenged schlemiel in his ill-fitting coat of armor that has been magnetized by a stroke of lightning draws as many laughs as he's drawn with his tongue twister. Seinfeld's verbal comedy in the sitcom bearing his name would have been less funny without his ungainly neighbor Kramer regularly crashing through his door. As if to put paid to my theory of slapstick as strictly goyish, when Joseph Gordon-Levitt (Jewish) was invited to host the popular television show *Saturday Night Live*, he performed in homage a dance routine modeled on O'Connor's "Make 'Em Laugh"—music and lyrics, I've neglected to mention, by Arthur Freed (Jewish) and Nacio Herb Brown (not).

In the same way that I once underappreciated the physical potential of Jewish comedy, I may have overestimated its refinement or, rather, the essential nature of its refinement. In a Yiddish joke on this subject, two Jews traveling by wagon along a narrow road see boulders blocking their path. They stop to consider what to do, and as they sit there, a wagon approaches carrying two peasants. The Gentiles get out, roll up their sleeves, and shove the rocks away. "There's goyish thinking for you," says one Jew to the other: "always with force." Historically speaking, at the point in the road where Jews began to take the measure of themselves in relation to their neighbors, they were constrained to recognize invidious features of the comparison; the joke was on them if they expected to get anywhere without putting shoulder to the boulder. Yet in telling this joke, even as it pokes fun at Jewish impracticality, Jewish self-mockery registers pride in its subtler and keener nature. Jewish humor grew coarser only once Jews got out of the wagon to get the job done themselves.

A decisive challenge to my association of refinement with Jewish humor came with the 2006 movie *Borat: Cultural Learnings of America for Make Benefit Glorious Nation of Kazakhstan*, in which the British comedian Sacha Baron Cohen stars as an anti-Semitic, misogynistic, homophobic, brutish Kazakh television reporter sent to report on life in the United States. A running in-joke of the film is Borat's Hebrew—the language he speaks with his fellow Kazakh producer Azamat Bagatov, who answers him in Armenian—which identifies this comedy as not simply "Jewish" but indeed learnedly so. Brooks had done something similarly incongruous when he had the American Indians of *Blazing Saddles* exchanging dialogue in Yiddish. But whereas Yiddish was the Jewish vernacular, and was still widely known to American Jews, Hebrew in a non-Israeli film is the language only of Jews who acquire it through study. This intimate signal to the educated

Jews in Cohen's audience had the effect of reassuring some of them that the filmmaker was a member of the tribe—and hence that all of Borat's anti-Semitic slurs, including that Jews caused 9/11, are there to expose the anti-Semites who hold such views.

By the same logic of comedy, the film's vulgarity is meant to expose vulgarity—and its *slapshtick* to make fun of slapstick. Borat and Azamat, arguing over the charms of a woman, fall into a naked wrestling match that exceeds in its loutishness any physical comedy ever filmed for a commercial feature film. If pornography uses nudity for sexual arousal, this anti-porn goes beyond impropriety and mere indecency, spoofing homoeroticism in the same way that Borat's anti-Semitism mocks anti-Semitism. Rude anti-Jewish behavior becomes a new form of Jewish comedy for viewers who are no longer bound by inhibitions of physical modesty.

Yiddish wit once mocked the illiteracy of Jewish culture in the United States—"If a *hazan* doesn't know Hebrew, they call him a cantor"—and the inauthenticity of its faith—"To us, it's a miracle if God does what the rabbi wants; to you, it's a miracle if the rabbi does what God wants." One might simply note in this connection that more so than other branches of culture, humor is a referendum on the actual. Abroad or in Israel, declining Jewish literacy (and observance) left Jewish comic writers with less indigenous material to work with. Whereas Jewish comedians of the Borscht Belt once delivered punch lines in Yiddish (not necessarily at its highest literary levels), the progressive evaporation of the language yielded only the thinnest residue of rude terms like putz, klutz, and schmuck. Analogously, whereas the comedians of the thirties and forties tried to keep the audience's mind off the genocide that was consuming their relatives in Europe, nowadays that genocide massacre is merely comic fodder. Hence Sarah Silverman's skit about her lesbian niece who "loves Hebrew school" and comes home with the information that Hitler killed sixty million Jews. When Aunt Sarah interjects, "I think you mean six million," the niece shrugs: "Whatever." Big laugh follows. Ostensibly intended to ridicule the contemporary Jew's miseducation, routines like these make it hard to distinguish the degeneracy of the mocker from the mocked.

■ Coping with Political Correctness

To be sure, vulgarity may also function as a mask from behind which it is safe to defy the norms of political correctness. Intimations of this turn in Jewish humor came to me one day in the late 1990s when a Harvard student of Yiddish literature told me that he had become a writer for *Beavis and Butt-Head*. I was incredulous. That animated television show features a pair of teenage goons whose all-around offensiveness exceeds the bounds of even bad taste. The student was an observant Jew, as far removed from coarseness as kosher cuisine is from pork. I asked him how he came to write for a show like that. He replied: "I was at Rabbi [Shlomo] Riskin's yeshiva in Efrat [Israel], and figured that writing at breakfast would not be considered *bitul Torah*." Translated as "neglecting the study of Jewish law," bitul Torah, or rather the avoidance of it, is an important precept of Judaism, and though obviously applied with different degrees of stringency to persons at different stages of life, is paramount for yeshiva students who come to master Jewish sources. The student explained how he had found the only time of day when Talmudic study could be briefly suspended without offending the priority of learning to which the institution was devoted. He did not think it necessary to account for *how come* a student of Torah would simultaneously be writing for that show, taking for granted what I found preposterous—namely, that a sensitive Jew and student of Torah might want to write dialogue for insensitive boors.

Originally associated with totalitarian societies that block dissenting views, political correctness leaches into democratic culture when the latter tries to impose a comparable conformism. "We can't open our mouths without being denounced as racists, misogynists, supremacists, imperialists, or fascists," wrote the U.S. Nobel Laureate Bellow in 1994, after being denounced as all of the above when he tried to make the point that only highly literate societies could have produced literary masterpieces: "Who is the Tolstoy of the Zulus? The Proust of the Papuans? I'd be glad to read him."[6] The outrage that greeted Bellow's quip suggests that anti–political correctness humor cannot speak freely in its own name but instead is more safely consigned to a mild racist like Archie Bunker in the television sitcom *All in the Family*. That show's condescension to Bunker is what allowed him to sound off against "spics," "Commies," and even "coloreds" with a frankness that would otherwise have been forbidden to any writer of the show. Beavis and Butt-head are likewise agents for unpopular views.

At the turn of the twenty-first century, the comedian Larry David, chief writer of the sweet-tempered *Seinfeld* series, designed for his new sitcom *Curb Your Enthusiasm* a version of the character "Larry David" (LD), who is as unmannered as Beavis and Butt-Head without their excuse of youth, and as heated as Archie Bunker without his excuse of invincible bias and ignorance. LD is an equal-opportunity offender. Tactless about a disabled person's entitlement to a handicap restroom, a lesbian's feminism, and a black man's touchiness about race, he makes children weep, friends disown him, his wife divorce him, and restaurateurs banish him from the premises. LD specializes in blasting Hollywood's liberal pieties—pieties that Hollywood has substituted for the religious devotions it thinks it has outgrown.

In one iconic episode of *Curb Your Enthusiasm*, a survivor of the Holocaust comes to dinner expecting to meet a fellow "survivor" and instead encounters a runner-up of *Survivor*, the television reality show. The transparent humor in the term's double entendre grows funnier as the two men compete in recounting their respective sufferings, with their machismo invested in how much each has overcome. The reality show contestant expounds on the deprivations he experienced in the Australian outback—he was reduced to wearing flip-flops! The tough old Jew's contempt for such a poor excuse for hardship detonates the whole convention of reality shows, but his participation in this sweepstakes of victimhood spoofs as well the catalog of horrors that has become a Jewish badge of honor. If American Jews have indeed reduced their cultural heritage to the Holocaust, and appear to congratulate themselves on the enormity of their loss, they deserve a satirist's derision. In a cyclic process, the ridicule coarsens Jewishness and a coarsened Jewishness invites ridicule.

The schlemiel—that once-familiar Jewish comic character—functioned as the underdog who pits his moral strength against the greater political and social powers of the surrounding majority. The schlemiel of Yiddish humor was an innocent—the soldier who, when ordered to charge the enemy with a bayonet, says, "Captain, please show me my man. Maybe we can come to an understanding." Finding another man in bed with his wife, the schlemiel refrains from waking the usurper lest he also wake the child in the adjoining crib—who turns out not to be his. In this same tradition, U.S. fictional characters, like the eponymous Gimpel the Fool (1945) by Isaac Bashevis Singer, Friedman's Stern (1962), Bellow's Herzog (1964), and Malamud's Fidelman (1969), interpret the perceived unmanliness of the Jewish male, the short guy in glasses, as a moral counterforce to a success-driven world. In many of the parts they played, Danny Kaye and Woody Allen exemplified the weakling who outmaneuvers the generals, the sucker who bests the sages, and the loser who wins the girl.

It was foolish of me to believe, as I once did, that having been refined to artistic perfection by Sholem Aleichem, reproduced ad infinitum in Jewish joking, and put to use by so many Jewish writers and producers, the schlemiel would have to be retired from Jewish comedy, like the coat in the song that is reduced as it gets worn down progressively to jacket, waistcoat, pocket, and button, until all that's left of it is the song about the process. Not at all! In came the Bulgarian Jewish novelist Angel Wagenstein's tragicomic novel of the "life of Isaac Jacob Blumenfeld through two world wars, three concentration camps, and five motherlands," which credits as its sources Sholem Aleichem and the whole repertoire of Jewish joking the way that the Talmud credits the Bible as *its* source. In came the Hungarian-born French writer Adam Biro's "autobiography" in the form of Jewish jokes that he claims have formed him to the point that telling them is his medium of self-revelation. And in came the young American Jewish novelist Joseph Skibell, who turns the credulous schlemiel of early twentieth-century Vienna into an eponymous "curable romantic," an ingenious term for the innocent whose life's journey takes him to Auschwitz. In these literary amalgams of history and invention, fiction and fact, the innocent schlemiel emerges durable, engaging, and morally intact.[7]

Very much in contrast, our television schlemiel LD *earns* the contempt in which he is held. He is now the Jew with influence, thoughtlessly rich. The transformation of this character from harmless to hurtful demonstrates the adjustment of Jewish humor to altered conditions of power and prosperity. Puncturing political correctness in liberal democracies is hardly as dangerous as defying Hitlerism or Stalinism in Europe, which may be why American Jewish comic heroes are no longer necessarily winsome or charming. The man who drives the slickest car on the road can't claim the naïveté of an eastern European Jew in his wagon, and the owner of the biggest house on the block can't garner the affection reserved for

Molly Goldberg yoo-hooing out of her cramped apartment window. From behind the mask of Hollywood success, the creator of LD exposes the foibles of a community that has no excuse for its moral failures.

■ One update, and I am done. In 2010, Howard Jacobson was awarded the Man Booker Prize, Britain's highest annual literary honor, for *The Finkler Question*, a funny study of the current war against the Jews in the birthplace of the Magna Carta. The book turns on the prickly friendship of three aging men—two Jews and a Gentile—who together probe "the Jewish question," which the non-Jew among them, Julian Treslove, has named for one of the two others, his old schoolmate Samuel Finkler. Finkler's Oxford degree in moral philosophy has given him the caché to write a series of "practical wisdom guides" with titles like *The Existentialist in the Kitchen* and *The Little Book of Household Stoicism*, whose commercial successes he has parlayed into minor celebrity as a television talking head. But the novel's point of view is that of the more pedestrian Treslove, and its satire is directed mostly at Samuel for the way he embodies the Finkler question.

Though the plot turns on mourning and love (as his name suggests, Treslove comes close to love without finding it), the novel's main comic target is Finkler's obsession with the criminal behavior he attributes to the nation-state of "Israyel" (sneer when you say it). Having joined the British elite, Finkler outdoes the anti-Jews among that class by taking up their hostility to Israel and blaming his fellow Jews for the aggression directed against them. He becomes the creative voice of

Britain's Ashamed Jews—a group whose logo he changes to "ASHamed Jews," which, he explains, "might or might not, depending on how others felt, be shortened now or in the future to *ASH*, the peculiar felicity of which, in the circumstances, he was sure it wasn't necessary for him to point out."[8] Needless to say, this group is chagrined not by any sins of its own but rather by Israel's alleged mistreatment of the Palestinians. ASH means that where the Nazis dared to go vis-à-vis the Jews, there go the Zionists vis-à-vis the Palestinian Arabs.

Like all good social satire, Jacobson's merely exaggerates what is real: in today's England, Jews are not vilified primarily as capitalists, Communists, or aliens but instead as claimants to their own country and its protection. Contributing to this assault are the political actions of anti-Israel Arabs and Muslims, the recycled anti-Jewish prejudice of a faded aristocracy, and democracy's recourse to a convenient scapegoat. At the time I write this, the British Academic and Cultural Movement of Boycott, Divestment, and Sanctions is trying to persuade the Shakespeare Festival to revoke its invitation to Israel's Habimah Theater to participate in a multinational commemoration. The fictional Finkler would be among such actual petitioners, for, as the narrator notes:

> To be an ASHamed Jew did not require that you had been knowingly Jewish all your life. Indeed, one among them only found out he was Jewish at all in the course of making a television program in which he was confronted on camera with *who he really was*. In the final frame of the film he was disclosed weeping before a memorial in

> Auschwitz to dead ancestors who until that moment he had never known he'd had. "It could explain where I get my comic genius from," he told an interviewer for a newspaper, though by then he had renegotiated his new allegiance. Born a Jew on Monday, he had signed up to be an ASHamed Jew by Wednesday and was seen chanting "We are all Hezbollah" outside the Israeli embassy on the following Saturday.[9]

With a single dart, Jacobson spears Holocaust exploitation—that by now perennial target of Jewish satire—and the Jew's floundering sense of identity in a declining culture attracted to fanatics who are secure in their cause. But Jacobson has chosen a doubly clever angle for his satire. Rather than taking on anti-Semitism outright, he targets the Jews who have aligned themselves with the anti-Jews. In doing so, he deflects his ridicule from British elites per se and toward the craven Jewish complicity with them. One is tempted to speculate that this is what allowed the Man Booker committee to award him its prize without implicating the cultural establishment, of which it is a representative, among the targets of his satire.

Be that as it may, let us also not overlook the ASHamed Jew's attribution of his "comic genius" to his newly discovered Jewishness. This know-nothing claims the license, as his birthright, to exploit for comedy what other Jews have been paying for with their lives. In the course of this book I have tried to highlight warnings against Jewish humor that issue from the best of its practitioners. Some, like Sholem Aleichem and Roth, have pointed out its injurious potential when used to excess. Others, in very different circumstances, have resorted to humor to redress a moral order disfigured by immoral regimes, and have been forcibly silenced by those whom their humor has exposed. *The Finkler Question* warns us that with the rise of anti-Israel aggression and concurrent slippage of Jewish confidence, a real-life ASHamed Jewish comic may soon be mocking the likes of Jacobson—and perhaps to no less critical and popular acclaim.

Always eager to "contribute" to the world around them, which was the long-standing precondition of their stay in other people's lands, Jews in modern times may want to claim humor among the blessings they share with and bestow on their fellow citizens. Returning us to where this book began, the cultural historian Michael Brenner asks, for example, what the history of humor in German would be without the poetry of Heine, anecdotes of Max Liebermann, films of Lubitsch, satires of Kurt Tucholsky, and so forth and so on, and on.[10] That these masters of German humor ended in exile and some in suicide, their works banned and burned by the masters of German politics, merely reinforces the benefits of tolerating laughter over its suppression, since what was better for the Jews would have been indubitably and incomparably also better for Germany. It is this correlation between Jewish humor and toleration that the Czech liberal Karbusicky celebrated as the hope for a better Europe.

Internally, among themselves, modern Jews took for granted the advantages of humor. Two old Jews meet in the Warsaw Ghetto, and one complains to the other of hunger, typhus, and people dying like flies: "Not one of us will survive to the end of the war." The second comforts him. "Don't worry. It's true that you won't survive, and I won't survive, but we will survive." Transcribed in February 1941, this would not make it into the 2012 Broadway review *Old Jews Telling Jokes*, though the underlying assumption—of a kind of enduring collective triumph over adversity of all descriptions—is as implicit in the jokes of the show as, mutatis very much mutandis, in those of the ghetto. Getting a joke may indeed be the last cultural bond among Jews headed for doom—or doomed to be Jews. Yet the German example also reminds us that Jewish humor, which has set the bar for moral self-correction and self-accountability, also sends a cautionary note. If Jews truly consider humor to have restorative powers, they ought to encourage others to laugh at themselves as well. Let Muslims take up joking about Muhammad, Arabs satirize jihad, British elites mock their glib liberalism, and anti-Semites spoof their politics of blame.

If the Jewish kind of laughter is truly wholesome, it ought to become universal fare. Until such time, Jews would do well to reexamine their brand and appreciate what it portends. One side laughing is not as harmless as one hand clapping.

Acknowledgments

My late teacher Uriel Weinreich identified anonymity as a distinguishing characteristic of folklore. Scholarship demands attribution, but folklore, a category emphatically embracing humor and joking, is a geyser that spouts for anyone with a handy pail. In this book I owe much to humorists whom I cannot identify; nor can I hope to credit all those whose ideas and information I have ingested.

Some thanks are straightforward. Harvard's libraries, and especially Widener's Judaica division headed by Charles Berlin, contain so much more relevant material than I was able to integrate that my gratitude for daily access to its treasures is riddled with anxiety over how much more might have been included. The National Yiddish Book Center and constituent units of the Center for Jewish History provide welcome access to documents and sources via the Internet. Special thanks to Jacob Wisse, director of the Yeshiva University Museum, for making the museum's resources available to me.

Among the kinds of materials I consulted are general studies of humor and humorists, specialized studies and anthologies of Jewish humor, studies of humor in other cultures with which Jews interacted, works on authors and texts discussed in this book, works on the emergence of comedy as a modern profession, and visual material, including art and photography, comics and caricature, film and video. Excepting English, Yiddish, Hebrew, French, and German, I am dependent on translation, so I owe special gratitude to those who have rendered into English the delights of other languages. My most humbling scholarly source in this project was Dov Sadan, the first professor of Yiddish at the Hebrew University of Jerusalem, who served in his own person as a veritable Jewish encyclopedia. Once, overwhelmed by his erudition, I asked how he succeeded in knowing so much; he replied that he gained at least two hours a day by not being able to read English.

I had help from former and present colleagues, including James Kugel, Jay Harris, Shaye Cohen, Bernard Septimus, Marion Aptroot, and Irit Aharony; excellent editorial advice from Werner Sollors; guidance from Hana Wirth-Nesher, Michael Brenner, Saul Morson, and Yossi Prager; jokes from Menahem Butler and Allan Nadler; and research assistance from Tom Connolly and, longer ago, Kyle Berkman. I borrowed from the cartoon collection posted on the office door of my Harvard colleague Jon Levenson, and drew inspiration from Bill Novak and Moshe Waldoks's tasteful *The Big Book of Jewish Humor*, which—dare I say?—rivals Nathan Ausubel's *Treasury of Jewish Folklore* (1948) and *Treasury of Jewish Humor* (1951). Moshe and Bill shared their experiences with my classes at Harvard on "The Comic Tradition in Jewish Culture," as did members of the Friars Club and the ever-generous Saul Bellow. Among my fellow professors of Yiddish, I owe special thanks to Justin Cammy and Jeremy Dauber, whose work on humor has been a great help to mine. It is my good fortune to have for a brother David G. Roskies, who shares my excitement over Yiddish and Jewish literature, suggests new directions, and inspires by creative example.

Heartfelt appreciation to graduate students and teaching fellows who contributed to this project over the years, including Debra Caplan, Ofer Dynes, Jessica Fechtor, Jennifer Heilbronner Munoz, Kelly Johnson, Alberto Ribas Casasayas, Sasha Senderovich, Miriam Udel, Asya Vaisman, Yuri Vedenyapin, and Sunny Yudkoff—with special thanks to Eitan Kensky and Dara Horn for their continuing feedback. I am hardly less grateful for the papers and insights of undergraduates in my classes, some of whom have gone on to distinguished careers in comedy. Ross Arbes kindly introduced me to the inner sanctum of the *Harvard Lampoon*, where I learned, what should not have surprised me, that its most fabled alumnus is my friend George Rohr.

Bellow's contribution to Jewish humor far exceeds its citations in these pages; I am grateful to Janis Bellow for her generous supervision of his legacy. Thanks to Ann Charney for constant encouragement, to Lida De Fougerolles for the trip to Prague, and to Gita Rotenberg and Jennifer Roskies for their funds of material. I am as fortunate in my friends as I am in family, and thank each in turn.

Since Fred Appel of Princeton University Press was the first person I proposed this project to years before I began writing the book, I was delighted that it landed in his capable hands. It has been a true pleasure to work with him along with Sarah David and everyone at the press. Inexpressible thanks to Arthur Fried, Mem Bernstein, and Roger Hertog for their publishing and cultural initiatives, including the Tikvah Fund's Library of Jewish Ideas, of which this volume forms a part.

Neal Kozodoy, editor of the Library of Jewish Ideas, oversaw the progress of this book from proposal to publication. Those who have enjoyed his editorial supervision will take me at my word when I credit him for everything sound in it; my book's shortcomings betray that he could only do so much. I could not have written this without his friendship.

Although *No Joke* exposes the threat of a hilarity that impedes effective communal self-protection, it also celebrates the Jewishness into which I was born and raised, and the joys of a Jewish home—ours—that has been an incubator of Jewish humor. Our children inherited the talent from their father, and have imported it into their own adult lives and acquired families with reciprocal give-and-take. I hope that Billy and Suzanne, Jacob and Rebecca, Abby and Ben reap as much joy and laughter from their children as they have brought to Len and me.

This book is dedicated with timeless gratitude to our adored grandchildren, Sonia, Maddy, Resa, Nate, Pearl, Camilla, and Claire, and to our step-grandson, Benjamin.

Notes

Introduction

1. Immanuel Olsvanger, ed., *Royte Pomerantsen: Jewish Folk Humor* (New York: Schocken, 1947), 3. This book and its companion volume, *L'Chayim* (New York: Schocken, 1949), are superior collections of Yiddish humor. Consisting of transcriptions of Yiddish originals into the roman alphabet, they also make effective teaching tools and invaluable guides to regional differences in pronunciation.
2. Sigmund Freud, *Jokes and Their Relation to the Unconscious*, trans. and ed. James Strachey (New York: W. W. Norton, 1960), 133.
3. Ibid., 95.
4. Ibid., 134.
5. Theodor Reik, *Jewish Wit* (New York: Gamut Press, 1962), 136. The phrase *Barukh atoh adonoy*, "Blessed art Thou, O Lord," is the opening formula of most Jewish blessings.
6. Arthur Schnitzler, *The Road into the Open*, trans. Roger Byers (Berkeley: University of California Press, 1992), 113.
7. William Novak and Moshe Waldoks, eds., *The Big Book of Jewish Humor: 25th Anniversary* (New York: HarperCollins, 2006), xxv.
8. Graham Turner, "Understanding the Jews," *Daily Telegraph*, April 10, 2001.
9. Novak and Waldoks, *The Big Book of Jewish Humor*, xlv.

10. Davies treats this aside as a categorical conclusion and "demonstrates" its "error" by citing self-critical joking among Scots in the late nineteenth century—without, however, comparing its proportion in the two cultures. See Christie Davies, "Undertaking a Comparative Study of Humor," in *The Primer of Humor Research*, ed. Victor Raskin (Berlin: Mouton de Gruyter, 2008), 175; Christie Davies, *The Mirth of Nations* (New Brunswick, NJ: Transaction, 2002), 51–75.
11. Elliott Oring, *Jokes and Their Relations* (New Brunswick, NJ: Transaction, 2010), 116. The footnote cites Hermann Adler, "Jewish Wit and Humor," *Nineteenth Century* 33 (1893): 457–69.
12. Leonard J. Greenspoon, ed., *Jews and Humor* (West Lafayette, IN: Purdue University Press, 2011).
13. Hillel Halkin, "Why Jews Laugh at Themselves," *Commentary* 121, no. 4 (April 2006): 47–54.
14. Ariela Krasney, *The Badkhan* [Hebrew] (Ramat-Gan: Bar Ilan University, 1998).
15. Heinrich Heine, "Prinzessin Sabbat," translated literally, with insightful discussion, by S. S. Prawer in *Heine's Jewish Comedy* (Oxford: Oxford University Press, 1983), 554–55. For a versified translation, see, for example, Heinrich Heine, "Princess Sabbath," trans. Aaron Kramer, in *The Poetry and Prose of Heinrich Heine*, ed. Frederic Ewen (New York: Citadel Press, 1948), 264.
16. See Mendele Mocher Sforim, *Di kliatshe*, trans. "The Mare," in Joachim Neugroschel, *The Great Works of Jewish Fantasy and Occult* (Woodstock, NY: Overlook, 1986): 545–663.
17. Lee Berk and Stanley Tan, interview in *Humor and Health Journal* (September–October 1996). Based on Lee Berk and Stanley Tan, "Neuroendocrine Influences of Mirthful Laughter," *American Journal of the Medical Sciences* 298 (October 1989): 390–96.
18. See "Laughter Is the Best Medicine," http://helpguide.org/life/humor_laughter_health.htm.

19. Sholem Aleichem, "The Haunted Tailor," trans. Leonard Wolf, in *The Best of Sholem Aleichem*, ed. Irving Howe and Ruth R. Wisse (Washington, DC: New Republic Books, 1979), 36.
20. Albert Goldman, *Ladies and Gentlemen—Lenny Bruce!!* (New York: Random House, 1974), 106.
21. Isaac Babel, "Gedali," in *Collected Stories*, trans. David McDuff (London: Penguin, 1994), 118.

■ 1. German Lebensraum

1. Theodor Herzl, *Old-New Land*, trans. Lotta Levensohn, preface Jacques Kornberg (Princeton, NJ: M. Wiener, 1997), 12. I have retained the spelling of names, minus the umlaut, in the quoted text.
2. Ibid., 173.
3. Sigmund Freud, *Jokes and Their Relation to the Unconscious*, trans. and ed. James Strachey (New York: W. W. Norton, 1960), 74–75, 137–38, 134. The last of these jokes appears as an episode in *King of the Schnorrers* (see chapter 3).
4. Ibid., 55.
5. Ibid., 133.
6. Freud proposed the English title "Man's Discomfort in Civilization" for *Das Unbehagen in der Kultur*, translated by James Strachey as *Civilization and Its Discontents* (New York: W. W. Norton, 1961). That Freud owed nothing to Herzl in his understanding of anti-Semitism is clear from this discussion of people's instinct for aggression:

   > The advantage which a comparatively small cultural group offers of allowing this instinct an outlet in the form of hostility against intruders is not to be despised. It is always possible to bind together a considerable number of people in love, so long as there are other people left over to receive the manifestations of their aggressiveness. . . . In this respect the Jewish people, scattered everywhere, have rendered most

useful services to the civilizations of the countries that have been their hosts. (Ibid., 61)

7. "Heinrich Heine is one of the most controversial figures in the history of German literature, some would argue *the* most controversial," observed George F. Peters (*The Poet as Provocateur: Heinrich Heine and His Critics* [Rochester, NY: Camden House, 2000], 1).
8. Heinrich Heine, "Ein Fichtenbaum," in *Sämtliche Gedichte*, ed. Bernd Kortlander (Stuttgart: Philipp Reclam jun, 1997), 94. For alternate translations, see Web site of Ralph Dumain, http://www.autodidactproject.org/other/heinepoem.html.
9. Translated by Emma Lazarus, http://www.autodidactproject.org/other/heinepoem.html.
10. Heinrich Heine, "The Baths of Lucca," in *Travel Pictures*, trans. Peter Wortsman (Brooklyn, NY: Archipelago Books, 2008), 125. Freud first drew my attention to this work.
11. The original here reads "ohne Furcht vor Mesallianz," that is, "without fear of misalliance."
12. Heine, "The Baths of Lucca," 100–101.
13. Ibid., 107.
14. Ibid., 104. The punning is obviously better in the original book, *Reisebilder* (Zurich: Diogenes Verlag, 1993), 332–33.
15. Freud's use of this quotation—and "appropriation of Heine's voice"—is analyzed by Sander Gilman as part of his study *The Jew's Body* (New York: Routledge, 1991), which also includes a discussion of how "the Jewish nose" and other features of Jewish physiognomy figured negatively in notions of identity.
16. Jefferson S. Chase, in his partial translation of "The Baths of Lucca," coins the term "goyraffes" to catch the flavor of the untranslatable pun; see his *Inciting Laughter: The Development of "Jewish Humor" in 19th Century German Culture* (Berlin: Walter de Gruyter, 2000), 270.
17. Heine, "The Baths of Lucca," 145.
18. Sigmund S. Prawer, *Heine's Jewish Comedy* (Oxford: Clarendon Press, 1983), 155.

19. Hans Mayer, "Der Streit zwischen Heine und Platen," in *Aussenseiter* (Frankfurt: Suhrkamp, 2007), 222.
20. Heine, "The Baths of Lucca," 160.
21. Werner Sollors, personal communication with author, June 8, 2012.
22. Heine, "The Baths of Lucca," 128.
23. Franz Kafka, "Ein Bericht für eine Akademie," in *Der Jude*, November 1917, translated as "A Report to an Academy" in Willa Muir and Edwin Muir, trans., *Selected Short Stories of Franz Kafka*, intro. Philip Rahv (New York: Modern Library, 1952). Of several additional translations, the latest and crispest is in Joyce Crick, trans., *A Hunger Artist and Other Stories*, intro. and notes Ritchie Robertson (Oxford: Oxford University Press, 2012), 37–45. Nonetheless, the quotations, except where indicated, are from the Muirs' translation.
24. Prawer, *Heine's Jewish Comedy*, 319.
25. Muir and Muir, *Selected Short Stories of Franz Kafka*, 169, 168.
26. Ibid., 176.
27. Ibid., 173.
28. Crick, *A Hunger Artist and Other Stories*, 45. The nature of the ape's "pleasure" in the half-trained chimpanzee is made much more explicit in this translation.
29. Nahman Syrkin, "Heinrich Heine, the Tragic Jewish Poet" [Yiddish, trans. from Hebrew], in *Heinrich Heine, Verk* (New York: Farlag Yidish, 1918), 1:7. Not surprisingly, as theorist and founder of labor Zionism, Syrkin puts forth a view of German Jewish humor that has something in common with Herzl's.

■ 2. Yiddish Heartland

1. Sholem Aleichem, "Two Anti-Semites," trans. Miriam Waddington, in *The Best of Sholem Aleichem*, ed. Irving Howe and Ruth R. Wisse (Washington, DC: New Republic Books, 1979), 116.

2. Selma H. Fraiberg, *The Magic Years: Understanding and Handling the Problems of Early Childhood* (1959; repr., New York: Fireside 1996), 18.
3. Carl Reiner and Mel Brooks, *The Complete 2000 Year Old Man* (Los Angeles, CA: Rhino Records, 1994), part 1.
4. Yosef Haim Brenner, "On Sholem Aleichem" (1946), in *Prooftexts* 6, no. 1 (January 1986): 17.
5. Joseph Perl, *Revealer of Secrets*, trans. with intro. and notes Dov Taylor (Boulder, CO: Westview Press, 1997), 25. Although Taylor draws heavily from the scholarship of those working directly with Perl's original Hebrew and Yiddish, his English translation constitutes the most thoroughgoing edition of the work to date.
6. Shloyme Ettinger's (1803–56) *Serkele*, published posthumously in 1861, became a showcase for actresses on the Yiddish stage.
7. Abraham Goldfaden, "The Two Kuni-Lemls," in *Landmark Yiddish Plays*, ed. Joel Berkowitz and Jeremy Dauber (Albany: State University of New York Press, 2006), 234 (act 2, scene 7).
8. I am indebted for this interpretation to Alyssa Quint, "Naked Truths," in *Arguing the Modern Jewish Canon: Essays on Literature and Culture . . .* (Cambridge, MA: Harvard University Press, 2008), 555.
9. Ora Wiskind-Elper, *Tradition and Fantasy in the Tales of Reb Nahman of Bratslav* (New York: State University of New York Press, 1998), 180.
10. The Kotsk homily can be found in Louis I. Newman, trans. and ed., *The Hasidic Anthology* (New York: Bloch, 1944), 499–500.
11. Paul Oppenheimer, *Till Eulenspiegel: His Adventures* (New York: Singer Routledge, 2001), 69–71.
12. "Ir zayt bavornt" [You are secured], in Ozer Holdes, ed., *Stories, Jokes, and Pranks of Hershl Ostropolier* [Yiddish], (Kiev: Melukhe farlag far di natsionale minderhaytn in USSR, 1941), 115–16. This collection, issued under Soviet aegis, sharpens the anticlerical and anti-"capitalist" bite of Hershele's humor. At the other extreme is the softened impression of Hershele in Ye-

hiel Yeshaia Trunk's fictional account of his youth, *The Merriest Jew in the World* [Yiddish] (Buenos Aires: Yidbukh, 1953).

13. Chaim Bloch, *Hersch Ostropoler, ein jüdischer Till-Eulenspiegel des 18. Jahrhunderts, seine Geschichten und Streiche* (Berlin: Harz, 1921), 10.
14. As it happens, the copy of the book of Isaiah discovered among the Dead Sea Scrolls spells the word with the letter *vav*, which would make bonayikh the correct reading. See David Flusser, *Judaism of the Second Temple Period*: (Grand Rapids, MI: William B. Eerdmans Publishing Co., 2007), 170. But the tradition distinctly presents this as a creative misreading.
15. My main sources for these anecdotes are Yehoshua Hana Ravnitzki, *Yidishe vitsn* [Jewish jokes] [Yiddish] (1921–22; repr., New York: Shklarski, 1950); Alter Druyanov, *Sefer habedikha vehakhidur* [Jewish jokes and humor] [Hebrew], 3 vols. (Tel Aviv: Dvir, 1939). Both of these books organize their material according to subject. Earlier I cite Immanuel Olsvanger's two edited collections: *Royte Pomerantsen: Jewish Folk Humor* (New York: Schocken, 1947); *L'Chayim* (New York: Schocken, 1949).
16. Ted Cohen, *Jokes* (Chicago: University of Chicago, 1999), 17.
17. Heard from, or rather seen performed by, Allan L. Nadler, Association for Jewish Studies conference, Boston, 2010.
18. Marvin S. Zuckerman and Gershon Weltman, trans., *Yiddish Sayings Mama Never Taught You* (Van Nuys, CA: Perivale Press, 1969). English translation published on facing pages with Ignatz Bernstein, ed., *Yidishe shprikhverter un redensarten* [Collection of coarse and vulgar sayings] (Leipzig, 1908).
19. Shirley Kumove, *More Words, More Arrows* (Detroit: Wayne State University Press, 1999), 24. See also her earlier collection, *Words Like Arrows: A Collection of Yiddish Folk Sayings* (Toronto: University of Toronto Press, 1984), and its bibliographic note.
20. One day my mother said to my husband, "You know, a son-in-law is like a button on an overcoat: it can fall off," leaving him

to wonder whether she was picking a fight or making a philosophical observation.

21. Sholem Aleichem, *The Letters of Menakhem-Mendl and Sheyne-Sheyndl and Motl the Cantor's Son*, trans. and intro. Hillel Halkin (New Haven, CT: Yale University Press, 2002), 24.
22. Sigmund Freud, *Jokes and Their Relation to the Unconscious*, trans. and ed. James Strachey (New York: W. W. Norton, 1960), 95.
23. Sholem Aleichem, "The Tenth Man," in *Tevye the Dairyman and the Railroad Stories*, trans. and intro. Hillel Halkin (New York: Schocken, 1987), 274–75.
24. Ibid., 278–79.
25. Ravnitzki, *Yidishe vitsn*, 28–29.
26. Ibid., 29.
27. Itzik Manger, "Abraham and Sarah," in *The World According to Itzik: Selected Poetry and Prose*, trans. and ed. Leonard Wolf (New Haven, CT: Yale University Press, 2002), 11.
28. Ibid., 43. "Lomir beyde antloyfn keyn vin/un lomir a khupe shteln." Itsik Manger, "Di elegye fun Fastrigosa," in *Medresh Itsik* (Jerusalem: Magnes Press of the Hebrew University, 1984), 147.
29. [Yitzhok] Bashevis, "Gimpel Tam," *Yidisher Kemfer*, no. 593 (March 30, 1945): 17–20. Translated by Saul Bellow for *Partisan Review* 20 (May 1953): 300–313. Bellow recounted that Singer turned down his offer to translate more of his fiction on the (perhaps tongue-in-cheek) explanation that people would attribute its accomplishment to the better-known translator.
30. A composite English version can be found under that title in Nathan Ausubel, ed., *A Treasury of Jewish Folklore* (New York: Crown Publishers, 1948), 327–31.
31. Sholem Aleichem, "The Haunted Tailor," trans. Leonard Wolf, in *The Best of Sholem Aleichem*, ed. Irving Howe and Ruth R. Wisse (Washington, DC: New Republic Books, 1979), 36. The tailor of the title "*Der farkishefter shnayder*" has been variously

translated as "enchanted" and "bewitched," harking back yet again to Heine's image of the Jew who is under an evil spell.

3. The Anglosphere

1. Music by Jule Styne, lyrics by Stephen Sondheim, book by Arthur Laurents; project of David Merrick and Ethel Merman. All were Jews.
2. Julian, *Contra Galilaeos*, in *Greek and Latin Authors on Jews and Judaism*, ed., intro., trans., and comm. Menahem Stern (Jerusalem: Israel Academy of Sciences and Humanities, 1976–84): 2:84.
3. Israel Zangwill, *The King of the Schnorrers*, illustrated by George Hutchison (1894; repr., London: Henry Pordes, 1998). References are to the following: Lord George Gordon (1751–93), British Member of Parliament, led the anti-Catholic riots, was excommunicated from the Church of England in 1786, and was suspected of madness when he converted to Judaism the following year; the shared trust of Christians in biblical prophecy allowed them to extend to Jews just enough civic rights to enrich their treasury; the *Gentleman's Magazine* (founded in 1731) opposed the "infidel alien" outright; the state did not recognize marriages and bequests executed according to Jewish religious law; and Primrose Day, April 19, named after Benjamin Disraeli's favorite flower, commemorates the death of that former prime minister in 1881. Had anyone prophesied that England would one day mourn its Jewish prime minister (albeit one whose family had converted), they would have been considered seditious. Yet William Pitt the Younger, who was prime minister during the action of the novel, was glad to take advice behind the scenes from another Jewish Benjamin—Goldsmid (1755–1808)—who helped finance England's military campaigns against France during the French Revolutionary Wars (1792–99). During Tevele Schiff's tenure as rabbi of London's Great Synagogue (1764–91), the mystic Samuel Falk

achieved notoriety by putting into the synagogue's doorposts magical inscriptions that were said to have saved the building from being destroyed by fire; a former choir boy of the synagogue named John Braham (who had changed his name from Abraham) composed a song for tenors called "The Death of Nelson," commemorating the naval hero who perished at the battle of Trafalgar in 1805.

4. Ibid., 2.
5. Ibid., 48.
6. Stephen Potter, *The Sense of Humour* (London: Max Reinhardt, 1954), 54.
7. Ibid., 51ff.
8. Richard Raskin, *Life Is Like a Glass of Tea: Studies of Classic Jewish Jokes* (Aarhus, Denmark: Aarhus University Press, 1992), 101–19.
9. Ibid., 109.
10. Saul Bellow, ed., *Great Jewish Short Stories* (New York: Dell, 1963), 12.
11. Ibid., 11–12. This joke may owe something to the quip attributed to Austrian satirist Moritz Saphir: "When I was a Jew, God could see me but I could not see Him. When I became a Catholic, I could see God, but He could not see me. Now that I am a Protestant, He can't see me and I can't see Him."
12. Leo Rosten, "Groucho: The Man from Marx," in *The Many Worlds of Leo Rosten* (New York: Harper and Row, 1964), 14–20.
13. Leo Rosten, *The Return of H*Y*M*A*N K*A*P*L*A*N* (New York: Harper, 1959), 58.
14. Leonard Q. Ross, *The Education of Hyman Kaplan* (New York: Harcourt, Brace and Company, 1937), 90.
15. Leo Rosten, *The Joys of Yiddish* (New York: McGraw-Hill, 1968), 93.
16. Irwin Richman, *Sullivan County Borscht Belt: Images of America* (Charleston, SC: Arcadia, 2001), 9.
17. Joey Adams with Henry Tobias, *The Borscht Belt* (New York: Bobbs-Merrill, 1966), 63, 68.

18. "Red Buttons Roasts Frank," video, http://www.youtube.com/watch?v=NyOoVWdUfRo.
19. Philip Roth, George Plimpton interview on *Portnoy's Complaint* (1969), reprinted in *Reading Myself and Others* (New York: Farrar, Straus and Giroux).
20. Philip Roth, *Portnoy's Complaint* (New York: Random House, 1969), 185.
21. From the 1975 film *Love and Death*.
22. Roth, *Portnoy's Complaint*, 257.
23. Roth, *Portnoy's Complaint*, 79.
24. William Novak and Moshe Waldoks, eds., *The Big Book of Jewish Humor: 25th Anniversary* (New York: HarperCollins, 2006). Jokes attributed to, respectively, Jonathan Katz and Joel Chasnoff.
25. See, for example, "Philip Roth and the Jews: An Exchange," *New York Review of Books*, November 14, 1974. The piece reproduces in full Syrkin's original letter to the editor in *Commentary*, March 1973—a response to Irving Howe's famously negative "Philip Roth Reconsidered," *Commentary*, December 1972. The exchanges between these Jewish intellectuals of the wartime generation and the U.S.-born writer trying to break new literary ground offer stark, poignant insight into the boundaries of humor among Jews themselves when they are separated by different historical experiences and cultural ideals.
26. Roth, *Portnoy's Complaint*, 81.
27. Ibid., 168.
28. Ibid., 36–37, 111–12.
29. Ibid., 76.
30. Ibid., 274.

■ 4. Under Hitler and Stalin

1. Shimen Dzigan, *The Impact of Jewish Humor* [Yiddish] (Tel Aviv: Orly, 1974), 124. I benefited from John Efron's essay, read in manuscript, "From Lodz to Tel Aviv: The Yiddish Political

Satire of Shimen Dzigan and Yisroel Shumacher," and Yuri Vedenyapin's dissertation "'Doctors Prescribe Laughter': The Yiddish Stand-up Comedy of Shimen Dzigan," Harvard University, 2008.

2. Cited by Rudolph Herzog as a prime example of German Jewish humor in *Dead Funny: Humor in Hitler's Germany*, trans. Jefferson Chase (Brooklyn, N.Y.: Melville House, 2011): 6.
3. Max Weinreich, *History of the Yiddish Language*, trans. Shlomo Noble with Joshua A. Fishman (New Haven, CT: Yale University Press, 2008): 1:181.
4. All examples, except where indicated, are taken from Nachman Blumental, *Words and Expressions of the Khurbn-period* [Yiddish] (Tel Aviv: I. L. Peretz Publishers, 1981).
5. Cited in ibid., 163; Samuel D. Kassow, *Who Will Write Our History? Emanuel Ringelblum, the Warsaw Ghetto, and the Oyneg Shabes Archive* (Bloomington: Indiana University Press, 2007), 256–57.
6. Kassow, *Who Will Write Our History?* 256–57.
7. Dzigan, *The Impact of Jewish Humor*, 183.
8. Jerry Z. Muller, "Why Do Jews Succeed?" Web site Project Syndicate: A World of Ideas, March 29, 2010, http://www.project-syndicate.org/commentary/why-do-jews-succeed-.
9. Yosef Guri, *Lomir hern gute bsures: Dictionary of Blessings and Curses* [Yiddish] (Jerusalem, 2005), 106.
10. Felix Mendelsohn, *The Jew Laughs: Humorous Stories and Anecdotes*, intro. A. A. Brill (Chicago: L. M. Stein, 1935), 173.
11. Many of these jokes are collected in David A. Harris and Izrail Rabinovich, eds., *The Jokes of Oppression: Humor of Soviet Jews* (Northvale, NJ: Jason Aronson, 1988). See also works on Russian humor by Emil A. Draitser, including his autobiographical *Shush! A Memoir: Growing Up Jewish under Stalin* (Berkeley: University of California Press, 2008), and other referenced works in these chapters. Nowadays, collections and studies of Russian *anekdoty* are keeping pace with those devoted to Jewish humor.

12. Nadezhda Mandelstam, *Hope against Hope: A Memoir*, trans. Max Hayward (New York: Atheneum, 1970), 14.
13. For illustrations of Sholem Aleichem, see Susan Tumarkin Goodman, ed., *Chagall and the Artists of the Russian Jewish Theater* (New Haven, CT: Yale University Press, 2009). The Jewish sources and subjects of Chagall's art are most thoroughly considered in Benjamin Harshav, *Marc Chagall and the Lost Jewish World: The Nature of Chagall's Art and Iconography* (New York: Rizzoli, 2006).
14. These jokes and versions of others cited in this chapter can be found in David Brandenberger, ed., *Political Humor under Stalin* (Bloomington, IN: Slavica Publishers, 2009), 3. This invaluable overview reminds us that study of the subject is still in its infancy.
15. This joke and the following in Harris and Rabinovich, *The Jokes of Oppression*, 41, 46.
16. James von Geldern and Richard Stites, eds., *Mass Culture in Soviet Russia: Tales, Poems, Songs, Movies, Plays, and Folklore, 1917–1953* (Bloomington: Indiana University Press, 1995), 212. The editors cull their anecdotes from five sources, but many can be found in or are clearly adapted from earlier collections of Yiddish humor.
17. Seth Graham, *Resonant Dissonance: The Russian Joke in Cultural Context* (Evanston, IL: Northwestern University Press, 2009), 60.
18. Ted Cohen, *Jokes* (Chicago: University of Chicago, 1999), 22. Cohen attributes this to Rabbi Elliot Gertel, but I have found and heard it elsewhere.
19. Harris and Rabinovich, *The Jokes of Oppression*, 126.
20. *Di zelmenyaner hobn oysgearbet in meshekh fun doyres an eygenem reyakh—a min veykhn gerukh fun tsugelegenem hey mit nokh epes*. Moshe Kulbak, *The Zelmenyaners*, trans. Hillel Halkin (New Haven, CT: Yale University Press, 2013), 4.
21. Ibid., 23.
22. Ibid., 38.

23. Ibid., 144.
24. Ibid., 265.
25. Isaac Babel, "Di Grasso," trans. Peter Constantine, in *The Complete Works of Isaac Babel*, ed. Nathalie Babel (New York: W. W. Norton, 2002), 699.
26. Ibid., 700.
27. Ibid., 702. A considerably soberer reading is offered by Gregory Freidin, "Fat Tuesday in Odessa: Isaac Babel's 'Di Grasso,'" reprinted in Harold Bloom, ed., *Isaac Babel* (New York: Chelsea, 1987), 199–214.
28. Isaac Babel, "Our Great Enemy: Trite Vulgarity," *Pravda*, August 25, 1934. Reprinted in Isaac Babel, *The Lonely Years, 1925–1939*, ed. Nathalie Babel, trans. Andrew R. MacAndrew and Max Hayward (New York: Farrar, Straus and Giroux, 1964), 396–400.
29. A total of about two hundred thousand individuals served time for this offense, according to Roy Medvedev. Cited in Graham, *Resonant Dissonances*, 8.
30. Jurek Becker, *Jacob the Liar*, trans. Melvin Korfeld (New York: Harcourt Brace Jovanovich, 1975), 92.
31. Sigmund Freud, *Jokes and Their Relation to the Unconscious*, trans. and ed. James Strachey (New York: W. W. Norton, 1960), 290.

■ 5. Hebrew Homeland

1. Joseph Telushkin, *Jewish Humor: What the Best Jewish Jokes Say about the Jews* (New York: Quill, 1998), 173. This is an excellent guide to Jewish joking.
2. Sholem Aleichem, "Chava," in *Tevye the Dairyman and the Railroad Stories*, trans. Hillel Halkin (New York: Schocken, 1987), 69.
3. Theodor Reik, *Jewish Wit* (New York: Gamut, 1962), 26.
4. Shimen Dzigan, *The Impact of Jewish Humor* [Yiddish] (Tel Aviv: Orly, 1974), 317.

5. *Mentshele*, the Yiddish diminutive of *mentsh*, was widely used in Yiddish literature, popularized by the 1864 novel of Mendele Mocher Sforim, *Dos kleyne mentshele* [The little man]. The present wordplay, coined by the Yiddish poet Abraham Sutzkever, follows the pattern of compression of Heine's "He treated me *famillionnairely*."
6. William Novak and Moshe Waldoks, eds., *The Big Book of Jewish Humor: 25th Anniversary* (New York: HarperCollins, 2006), 137.
7. Shmuel Yosef Agnon, *In the Heart of Seas*, trans. I. M. Lask (New York: Schocken, 1947), 72.
8. Ibid., 20–21. I have slightly modified the translation.
9. Gershom Scholem, "S. Y. Agnon: The Last Hebrew Classic?" in *Commentary* 67 (1966). The article was a review of Agnon's *A Guest for the Night*.
10. S. Y. Agnon, speech, city hall, Stockholm, December 10, 1966, http://www.nobelprize.org/nobel_prizes/literature/laureates/1966/agnon-speech.html.
11. Elliott Oring, *Israeli Humor: The Content and Structure of the Chizbat of the Palmah* (Albany: State University of New York Press, 1981), 180–81. Most of this collection is culled and translated from Dan Ben Amotz and Haim Hefer, *Yalkut hakezavim* [Hebrew: A pack of lies] (Tel Aviv: Metsiut, 1979). I have made slight changes to the translation.
12. Oring, *Israeli Humor*, 156. For Oring's discussion, see ibid., 71.
13. *Bemedinat Hayehudim* [In the land of the Jews: Israeli humor in the 20th century], directed by Gavriel Bibliyovits et al., eleven-part series (Tel Aviv, Matar Plus, 2006).
14. See, for example, Edna Ofek and Ira Cahanman, "Humor as a Common Denominator in Immigrant Society" [Hebrew], in *Bikoret Ufarshanut* 21 (December 1986): 69–85.
15. Judges' statement, http://cms.education.gov.il/EducationCMS/Units/PrasIsrael/Tashas/Hagashas/NimukeiAshoftimGashash.htm. Professor Aliza Shenhar served as committee chair. For a coffee-table anthology of the comedy group's most popu-

lar expressions, see Gavri Banai, *Az ma haya lanu sham?* [All-time favorite phrases of the Gashash] (Ben-Shemen: Modan, 2004).

16. *Givat halfon eina ona* [Hill Halfon doesn't answer], written by Assi Dayan and Naftali Alter, directed by Assi Dayan (1976).
17. Ibid.
18. Limor Shifman, *Televised Humor and Social Cleavages in Israel* [Hebrew] (Jerusalem: Magnes of the Hebrew University, 2008), 111. See especially chapter 4.
19. Ofra Nevo and Jacob Levine, "Jewish Humor Strikes Again: The Outburst of Humor in Israel during the Gulf War," *Western Folklore* 53, no. 2 (April 1994): 145.
20. Ofra Nevo, "The Psychological Contribution of Humor in Israel during the Gulf War" [Hebrew], *Israel Journal of Psychology and Related Sciences* 1994 (4): 41–50..
21. Franz Kafka, diary entry, October 24, 1911, in *Diaries, 1910–1913*, trans. Joseph Kresh (New York, Schocken, 1948), 111.
22. Amir Gutfreund, *Our Holocaust*, trans. Jessica Cohen (New Milford, CT: Toby Press, 2006), 3.
23. Ibid., 4.

Conclusion

1. Vladimir Karbusicky, *Jewish Anecdotes from Prague*, trans. David R. Beveridge (Prague: V Ráji, 2005), 14–15.
2. Ibid., 11.
3. Ibid., 96–97.
4. Sigmund Freud, *Jokes and Their Relation to the Unconscious*, trans. and ed. James Strachey (New York: W. W. Norton, 1960), 131.
5. Henri Bergson, "Laughter," in *Comedy*, intro. and ed. Wylie Sypher (Garden City, NY: Doubleday, 1956), 84.
6. Saul Bellow, "Op-Ed: Papuans and Zulus," *New York Times*, March 10, 1994.

7. Angel Wagenstein, *Isaac's Torah*, trans. (from Bulgarian) Elizabeth Frank and Deliana Simeonova (New York: Handsel Books, 2008); Adam Biro, *Two Jews on a Train*, trans. (from French) Catherine Tihanyi (Chicago: University of Chicago Press, 2001); Joseph Skibell, *A Curable Romantic* (Chapel Hill, NC: Algonquin Books, 2010).
8. Howard Jacobson, *The Finkler Question* (London: Bloomsbury, 2010), 115.
9. Ibid., 138–39.
10. Michael Brenner, "When Humor was Still at Home in Germany" [German], in *Humor*, ed. Gisela Dachs (Frankfurt am Main: Suhrkamp, 2004), 13. To Heine, Liebermann, Lubitsch, and Tucholsky, Brenner adds the caricatures of Thomas Theodor Heine, reviews of Alfred Kerr, revues of Friedrich Hollaender, literary parodies of Robert Neumann, political lyrics of Erich Mühsam and Walter Mehring, critical writings of Karl Kraus, reportage of Egon Erwin Kisch, aphorisms of Peter Altenberg, cabaret numbers of Fritz Grünbaum, Anton Kuh, Mynona, Roda Roda, Peter Hammerschlag, and Fritz Kalmar—as well as the studies of jokes by Freud and Reik.

Index

Index